What A Life!

Stories of Amazing People

Longman

Milada Broukal

What A Life!: Stories of Amazing People, High Beginning

© 2001 by Addison Wesley Longman, Inc.
A Pearson Education Company.
All rights reserved.
No part of this publication may be reproduced,
stored in a retrieval system, or transmitted
in any form or by any means, electronic, mechanical,
photocopying, recording, or otherwise,
without the prior permission of the publisher.

Pearson Education, 10 Bank Street, White Plains, NY 10606

Vice president, director of publishing: Allen Ascher
Editorial director: Louisa Hellegers
Acquisition editor: Laura Le Dréan
Senior development manager: Penny Laporte
Development editor: Andrea Bryant, Cheryl Pavlik
Vice president, director of design and production: Rhea Banker
Associate director of electronic production: Aliza Greenblatt
Executive managing editor: Linda Moser
Production manager: Liza Pleva
Production editor: Martin Yu
Senior manufacturing manager: Patrice Fraccio
Senior manufacturing buyer: Dave Dickey
Photo research: Marianne Carello
Cover design: Elizabeth Carlson
Cover credits: Mountain climber: Solstice Photography/Artville; Violinist: Eye Wire Photography; Soccer ball/player: Eye Wire Photography; Writer: Eye Wire Photography; Scientist: Comstock
Text design: Elizabeth Carlson
Text composition: Publication Services, Inc.
Photo credits: p. 1, © Archivo Iconografico, S.A./CORBIS; p. 6, Hulton Getty/Liaison Agency; p. 11, © Bettmann/CORBIS; p. 16, © Bettmann/CORBIS; p. 21, © Bettmann/CORBIS; p. 26, © Bettmann/CORBIS; p. 31, National Park Service, U.S. Department of the Interior; p. 36, © Bettmann/CORBIS; p. 41, Special collections, California Polytechnic State University; p. 46, Photo by Tynan Bros, Jersey. Courtesy of Bishop Museum; p. 51, © Bettmann/CORBIS; p. 56, Archive Photos; p. 61, © Bettmann/CORBIS; p. 66, © Bettmann/CORBIS; p. 71, © Bettmann/CORBIS; p. 76, © Bettmann/CORBIS; p. 81, © Bettmann/CORBIS; p. 86, Copyright © Honda Motor Co., Ltd. All rights reserved.; p. 91, © Bettmann/CORBIS; p. 96, © Lucien Aigner/CORBIS; p. 101, © Owen Franken/CORBIS; p. 106, AP/Wide World Photos; p. 111, © Michael S. Yamashita/CORBIS; p. 116, AP/Wide World Photos

Library of Congress Cataloging-in-Publication Data

Broukal, Milada.
    What a life!: stories of amazing people / by Milada Broukal.
       p.   cm.
    Contents: [2] High Beginning
    ISBN: 0-201-61997-0 (v. 2)
    1. English language—Textbooks for foreign speakers. 2. Biography—
Problems, exercises, etc. 3. Readers—Biography. I. Title.

PE1128.B716   2000
428.6'4—dc21   99-059443

3 4 5 6 7 8 9 10—VHG—05 04 03 02 01

CONTENTS

INTRODUCTION

What A Life! Stories of Amazing People is a high beginning reader. It is the second in a three-book series of biographies for students of English as a second or foreign language. Twenty-four people have been selected for this book: 12 women and 12 men. Their backgrounds and talents are very different, ranging from a nineteenth-century English writer, to a Hawaiian princess, to a Native American sports hero. All of them have made significant contributions to the world.

Each unit focuses on one person's biography. The biographies have been arranged in chronological order; however, they can be taught in any order.

Each unit contains:

- A prereading activity
- A reading passage (650–700 words)
- Topic-related vocabulary work
- Comprehension exercises, including pair work
- Discussion questions
- A writing activity

BEFORE YOU READ opens with a picture of the person featured in that unit. Prereading questions follow. Their purpose is to motivate students to read, encourage predictions about the content of the reading, and involve the students' own experiences when possible. Vocabulary can be presented as the need arises.

The **READING** passage should be first done individually, by skimming for the general content. The teacher may wish to explain the bolded vocabulary words at this point. The students should then do a second, closer reading. Further reading(s) can be done aloud.

The two **VOCABULARY** exercises focus on the bolded words in the reading. *Meaning*, a definition exercise, encourages students to work out the meanings from the context. The second exercise, *Use*, reinforces the vocabulary further by making students use the words in a meaningful, yet possibly different, context. This section can be done during or after the reading phase, or both.

There are several **COMPREHENSION** exercises. Each unit contains *Understanding the Reading, Remembering Details,* and *Making Inferences.* All confirm the content of the text either in general or in detail. These exercises for developing reading skills can be done individually, in pairs, in small groups, or as a class. It is preferable to do these exercises in conjunction with the text, since they are not meant to test memory. These exercises are followed by *Tell the Story,* which is a spoken pair work activity where students can correct each other's mistakes.

DISCUSSION questions encourage students to bring their own ideas and imagination to the related topics in each reading. They can also provide insights into cultural similarities and differences.

WRITING provides the stimulus for students to write simple sentences about their own lives. Teachers should use their own discretion when deciding whether or not to correct the writing exercises.

What A Life! is an exciting introduction to some of history's most amazing people. Teachers may want to support their discussions with other books, magazine and newspaper articles, or videos. There are also many good websites, three of which are listed below. These sites are very informative, yet easy to navigate. They will be excellent resources for students and teachers alike.

www.encarta.com is a general, online encyclopedia.

www.biography.com is a website that specializes in biographies.

www.pathfinder.com/time/time100.com features profiles of *Time* magazine's choices for the "100 Most Important People of the 20th Century." Two of the people in this book—Louis Armstrong and Mother Teresa—were among those that were chosen.

UNIT 1

WOLFGANG AMADEUS MOZART
(1756–1791)

BEFORE YOU READ

Wolfgang Amadeus Mozart was one of the greatest composers of all time. He was famous and wrote hundreds of beautiful works during his lifetime.

Discuss these questions with a partner.

1. At what age do you think a child can learn to play a musical instrument?
2. What is your favorite kind of music?
3. Look at the picture of Wolfgang Amadeus Mozart. What can you say about him?

Now read about Wolfgang Amadeus Mozart.

WOLFGANG AMADEUS MOZART

Wolfgang Amadeus Mozart was a musical genius. He was born in 1756 in Salzburg, Austria. His father, Leopold, was a musician. He taught Wolfgang and his sister Maria Anna to play musical instruments. Wolfgang started to play the piano when he was only three years old. One day, Leopold and some musicians were playing a piece of music. Wolfgang was listening to them. After they finished, he started to play the violin part exactly as he had heard it. Wolfgang remembered the music after hearing it just once! Soon Leopold **realized** that it was impossible to teach his son music because Wolfgang knew almost everything already.

Wolfgang wrote his first piece of music for the piano when he was five years old. When he was six, he was already earning money for his family. He played for kings and queens and other important people. They paid a lot of money to hear him. He wrote his first symphony at the age of eight and his first opera at age 11. People called him the "wonder child." Wolfgang liked the attention. He worked hard and traveled a lot, but he was often sick.

Mozart was **cute** as a child. He had red cheeks and bright, blue eyes. But as he got older, he was not handsome. He was a small man with a large head and **pale** skin. He was always worried about his appearance. He liked to wear **elegant** clothes. He also took special care of his hair, which he thought was his best **feature.**

Mozart fell in love with his landlady's daughter. She did not love him, so he married her sister, Constanze. Constanze was very much like her husband. She was musical and loved to have fun. Unfortunately, the Mozarts had money problems. Wolfgang made a lot of money, but he **was** always **in debt.** Sometimes people didn't pay him with money; they gave him watches or jewelry instead. But when he got money, he usually spent it on expensive clothes and furniture. One story said that once when Mozart had no money to heat his house, he danced with his wife to keep warm. The Mozarts had six children, but only two lived to be adults.

Mozart worked very hard. He liked to work when it was quiet in the house. He began work at six o'clock in the evening and worked all night. He liked to write music while he was standing. He often slept for only four hours a night. He also worked very quickly. He wrote three of his greatest works in only six weeks. He also wrote a whole opera in just a few weeks. Many people believe that Mozart wrote faster than any other composer in history. Mozart also had the ability to write all kinds of music. He wrote operas, symphonies, and church music. And he wrote music for every instrument. He even wrote music for clocks. In all, Mozart wrote over 600 pieces of music.

Mozart died at the age of 35. No one really knows how he died. Some people believe someone **poisoned** him. Others say that he had a **weak** heart. Sadly, no one went to his funeral. They buried him as a poor person in a grave with no name. No one knows where his body is to this day.

VOCABULARY

◆ MEANING

What is the best meaning of the underlined words? Circle the letter of the correct answer.

1. Wolfgang Amadeus Mozart thought his hair was his best <u>feature</u>.
   a. something that people don't notice
   b. something that people notice
   c. something that is long

2. Mozart <u>was</u> always <u>in debt</u>.
   a. gave money to the poor
   b. had a lot of money
   c. owed money to people

3. Mozart's father <u>realized</u> his son had musical ability.
   a. hoped
   b. didn't think
   c. began to understand

4. Some people think that someone <u>poisoned</u> Mozart.
   a. gave him something to eat or drink to kill him
   b. was in a bad accident with him
   c. said bad things about

5. Mozart was a <u>cute</u> child.
   a. pretty
   b. clean
   c. unhappy

6. Mozart wore <u>elegant</u> clothes.
   a. old and dirty
   b. new and colorful
   c. stylish and beautiful

7. Some people say that Mozart had a <u>weak</u> heart.
   a. small
   b. not strong
   c. very sick

8. Mozart had <u>pale</u> skin.
   a. dark
   b. very thin
   c. without much color

◆ USE

Work with a partner and answer these questions. Use complete sentences.

1. What do you think a *cute* child looks like?
2. Why do you think a lot of people *are in debt*?
3. Where do people usually wear *elegant* clothes?
4. What do you think is your best *feature*?
5. What colors are *pale*? What colors are bright? Which do you like?
6. What kinds of things can be *weak*?

COMPREHENSION

◆ UNDERSTANDING THE READING

Circle the letter of the best answer.

1. As a child, Wolfgang Amadeus Mozart _____.
   a. didn't want to take   b. had a great talent   c. played one instrument
      music lessons   for music

2. Mozart became successful _____.
   a. at a young age   b. after he was married   c. later in life

3. When Mozart worked, he _____.
   a. wanted people   b. created a lot of work   c. only wrote for a few
      around him   in a short time   hours every night

◆ REMEMBERING DETAILS

Reread the passage and answer the questions.

1. Who was Mozart's first teacher?
2. How old was Mozart when he wrote his first piece of music?
3. What did Mozart look like as an adult?
4. Why did Mozart marry Constanze instead of her sister?
5. At what time did Mozart begin to work?
6. How many pieces of music did Mozart write?

◆ MAKING INFERENCES

When you make an *inference*, you decide something based on information that you already know. What inferences can you make about Mozart based on what you read in the story? Read these sentences. Circle *T* if the sentence is true and *F* if it is false. Then, underline one sentence in the passage that supports your answer.

	True	False
1. Mozart had the same kind of childhood as most people.	T	F
2. Mozart was careful with his money.	T	F
3. Mozart had very few friends.	T	F

◆ TELL THE STORY

Work with a partner. Tell the story of Wolfgang Amadeus Mozart to your partner. Use your own words. Your partner can ask you questions about the story. Then, your partner tells you the story and you ask questions.

DISCUSSION

Discuss the answers to these questions with your classmates.

1. What amazing people do you know?
2. When do you like to listen to music?
3. Mozart was successful in his lifetime, but he died without money or friends. What do you think about this?

WRITING

On a separate piece of paper, write six sentences or a short paragraph. Describe your work schedule. What days do you work? What time do you begin and end work?

Example: *I start work at 8 o'clock every day except Saturdays and Sundays.*

UNIT 2

DR. JAMES BARRY
(1795–1865)

BEFORE YOU READ

Dr. James Barry was the first woman in England to attend medical school and become a doctor.

Discuss these questions with a partner.

1. Who are some great people in medicine?
2. What are some recent discoveries in medicine?
3. Would you like to be a doctor? Why or why not?

Now read about Dr. James Barry.

DR. JAMES BARRY

Dr. James Barry was the first woman in England to go to medical school. When she was growing up, women could not go to medical school. So how did she become a doctor? She simply **pretended** that she was a man.

No one knows Dr. Barry's real name, her birth date, or her family's background. Some records show that she was born in 1795 in London. Some people say she was the daughter of a rich man or a royal prince. One fact we know is that in 1810, James Barry became a medical student at the University of Edinburgh.

James Barry's classmates **made fun of** her because she didn't have a beard and she was only five feet tall. But no one thought she was a girl. At the age of 20, James Barry graduated from the University of Edinburgh as a Doctor of Medicine. She was one of the youngest students to complete her studies. Dr. Barry then went to work in a London hospital and studied **surgery**. A year later, she entered the army and became a hospital assistant. We will never know how she avoided the army physical exam.

For the next 45 years, Dr. James Barry was a British officer and a successful surgeon. Everyone admired her. She began to do a lot of important work for the army. At that time, England had many **colonies** around the world. Dr. Barry spent a lot of time in foreign countries. She traveled to India, Corfu, Malta, and Jamaica. In 1856 she went to South Africa, and she was soon known as the best doctor and surgeon in the colony. She saved the life of the governor's daughter, and later she became the governor's personal doctor. People admired Dr. Barry, but she also had a **reputation** as a troublemaker. If people talked about her high voice or tiny figure, she became very angry. She was an excellent swordsman, and she started fights often.

Her work also got her in trouble. Dr. Barry wanted the highest medical **standards.** She made hospitals follow strict rules for taking care of the sick. She reported prison officials if they treated prisoners badly. She made many important changes, but she also made many enemies. Sometimes the army supported her and sometimes it didn't. Once there was even a **trial** for Dr. Barry because she did not obey orders.

Some people did not agree with Dr. Barry, but they always admired her as a doctor and a surgeon. However, some also thought the doctor was very strange. For example, she always dressed behind closed doors. In fact, she often shared rooms with male officers. She asked them to leave the room when she dressed.

In 1857, at the age of 62, Dr. Barry became Inspector General and moved to Canada. There, she worked to improve the soldiers' living conditions and get better food for them. In 1859, Dr. Barry became ill with the flu and went back to England to retire. She was very lonely after that. She died in 1865 at the age of 71.

An army doctor looked at the body quickly and simply said that Dr. Barry was dead. Later, someone discovered she was a woman. The secret was out, but the army never made an official announcement about its female officer. They buried Dr. Barry as a man. The details of Dr. Barry's life and the **sacrifices** she made died with her.

VOCABULARY

◆ MEANING

What is the best meaning of the underlined words? Circle the letter of the correct answer.

1. In the nineteenth century, England had many <u>colonies</u>.
   - a. countries England fought with
   - b. countries under England's control
   - c. countries that England sold things to

2. Dr. James Barry wanted the highest medical <u>standards</u>.
   - a. position of importance
   - b. level of quality
   - c. type of information

3. Dr. Barry had a <u>reputation</u> as a troublemaker.
   - a. the opinions others had of her
   - b. way of acting
   - c. the things that others did for her

4. Dr. Barry <u>pretended</u> that she was a man.
   - a. acted in a way that was not true
   - b. didn't want to be
   - c. talked about herself all the time

5. Dr. Barry made many <u>sacrifices</u> to be a doctor.
   - a. strong desires
   - b. important things she gave up
   - c. orders she gave to people

6. There was a <u>trial</u> for Dr. Barry because she did not follow orders.
   - a. when the police ask questions about a crime
   - b. when somebody goes to jail
   - c. when a court of law decides whether somebody did a crime

7. Dr. Barry's classmates <u>made fun of</u> her.
   - a. enjoyed spending time with her
   - b. joked about her in an unkind way
   - c. thought she was funny

8. She studied <u>surgery</u> in a London hospital.
   - a. medical treatment for men only
   - b. medical treatment where a doctor gives medicine to a patient
   - c. medical treatment where a doctor cuts open a patient's body

◆ USE

Work with a partner and answer these questions. Use complete sentences.

1. What kind of *reputation* do you want to have?
2. What are some types of *surgeries* that doctors perform?
3. Why do people often *pretend*?
4. Why do some people *make fun of* others?
5. What are some *standards* that your favorite restaurant has?
6. What country has or had *colonies*?

COMPREHENSION

◆ UNDERSTANDING THE READING

Circle the letter of the best answer.

1. When Dr. James Barry studied at the University of Edinburgh, she was _____.
   - a. a very bad student
   - b. treated badly because she was a woman
   - c. laughed at because she looked different

2. People thought that Dr. Barry _____.
   - a. was loved for her kindness and concern for others
   - b. was an excellent doctor but was not very likeable
   - c. did not do anything to make people notice her

3. When Dr. Barry wanted to improve the health of the soldiers, _____.
   - a. she was only following orders
   - b. she often got into trouble
   - c. people loved her for her good work

◆ REMEMBERING DETAILS

Reread the passage and answer the questions.

1. At what age did James Barry graduate from the University of Edinburgh?
2. For how many years was Dr. Barry a British officer?
3. Where did she go in 1856?
4. Why did Dr. Barry become the governor's personal doctor?
5. What kind of reputation did Dr. Barry have?
6. Why was there a trial for Dr. Barry?

◆ MAKING INFERENCES

Circle *T* if the sentence is true and *F* if it is false. Then, underline one sentence in the passage that supports your answer.

	True	False
1. Dr. Barry was less successful than the male doctors of her time.	T	F
2. Dr. Barry cared a lot about her patients.	T	F
3. Dr. Barry was afraid to disagree with people.	T	F

◆ TELL THE STORY

Work with a partner. Tell the story of Dr. James Barry to your partner. Use your own words. Your partner can ask you questions about the story. Then, your partner tells you the story and you ask questions.

DISCUSSION

Discuss the answers to these questions with your classmates.

1. Would you do something strange to get something you want? Give examples.
2. How have conditions changed for women since Dr. James Barry's times?
3. How do you think medicine will change in the future?

WRITING

On a separate piece of paper, write six sentences or a short paragraph. Describe a medical problem and its treatment.

Example: *My mother has a problem with her blood pressure. She takes medicine for it every day.*

UNIT 3
CHARLES DICKENS
(1812–1870)

BEFORE YOU READ

Charles Dickens was a famous and successful English writer of the nineteenth century. Many of his books are still popular today.

Discuss these questions with a partner.

1. Who is your favorite writer? What is your favorite book?
2. What kind of writing do you like best: poetry, novels, magazines, or newspapers?
3. Look at the picture of Charles Dickens. What can you say about him?

Now read about Charles Dickens.

CHARLES DICKENS

Charles Dickens was born in 1812 in Portsmouth, England. He was the second of eight children. His father always had problems with money. When Charles was 12 years old, his father went to prison because he was in debt. Charles had to leave school to help his family. He got a job putting **labels** on bottles of shoe polish in a dirty, old factory. Charles Dickens never forgot his difficult childhood. Many of his stories and books were about poor people and their problems.

Later, Charles went back to school for two more years. He left school when he was 15 years old to become a newspaper reporter. In 1836, he began to write *The Pickwick Papers.* It was published as a **series** and was a huge success. By age 24, Dickens was a famous writer in both Great Britain and the United States.

Many people bought his books, but they also paid to hear him read his stories aloud. Because there was no radio or television, people liked to hear famous writers read in public. Dickens read his work like he was acting in a play. He went on very successful reading tours and earned a lot of money.

Dickens was **meticulous.** Everything had to be just right. When he worked at home, everything had to be in its place. He worked at a desk by a window that always had a vase of flowers and the same **ornaments** on it. He wrote 2,000 words a day, and he **required** complete quiet while he wrote. He divided his page into three parts, and on each side he had notes in different colors. The main writing was in the middle, the story notes were in the right **margin**, and the chapter notes were in the left margin. He also cared a lot about his appearance. Dickens had many mirrors in his home. He combed his hair very often, even at dinner parties! He wore showy clothes, such as red velvet jackets, and he always had many rings on his fingers. He usually looked overdressed.

Dickens was **superstitious.** He thought that Fridays were lucky, and he touched certain things three times for luck. He always slept with his bed in a north-south position. When he spoke in public, he didn't want anyone to sit behind him. Everything around him had to be red, including the table and the carpet.

Dickens married Catherine Hogarth in 1836. They did not get along very well, and after 16 years of marriage they separated. Charles and Catherine had 10 children. After the separation, the younger children lived with Charles. Catherine's sister, Georgina, moved in with them and helped Charles manage the house.

Dickens always worked hard. When he was home, he followed a daily **routine.** He got up at seven o'clock, had breakfast at eight, and then worked until two in the afternoon. After that, he had a small lunch and worked or rode his horse until five o'clock. Then he had supper. After supper, he wrote again or went to the theater. He went to bed at midnight.

Dickens liked to make money. Because of his difficult childhood, he was afraid to be poor. In 1867, he began a long reading tour. He traveled throughout Europe and the United States. The trip was very tiring, and he became ill. Two years after he returned home, he died at the age of 58.

Charles Dickens wrote powerful and honest stories about the lives of poor people. The government even passed laws to stop some of the horrible things he wrote about in his books. Books like *David Copperfield, Great Expectations, Oliver Twist,* and *A Christmas Carol* were popular when Dickens wrote them, and they are still popular today.

VOCABULARY

◆ MEANING

Write the correct words in the blanks.

superstitious	meticulous	labels	required
ornaments	routine	margin	series

1. Most products have _____ that describe what they are and give other information about them.

2. Charles Dickens _____ special things when he wrote. He needed everything to be a certain way.

3. Dickens wrote in the space on the side of the page. His notes were in the _____.

4. Dickens was a _____ man because he believed in luck.

5. Stories in a _____ come one after the other in a certain order.

6. Dickens liked _____ on his desk. They were beautiful but not useful.

7. Dickens had a certain _____, so he did things the same way every day.

8. Dickens was very _____. Everything was always exactly right.

◆ USE

Work with a partner and answer these questions. Use complete sentences.

1. What do *labels* on products usually tell you?
2. What *ornaments* do you have in your home?
3. Are you a *superstitious* person? Explain.
4. What are some things you *require* when you work?
5. What are some things that *meticulous* people do?
6. What is your daily *routine*?
7. What is your favorite television *series*?

COMPREHENSION

◆ UNDERSTANDING THE READING

Circle the letter of the best answer.

1. As a child, Charles Dickens _____.
   - a. had many chances for success
   - b. thought only of himself
   - c. was very poor

2. In his daily life, Dickens _____.
   - a. was not a very nice person
   - b. liked to do things differently all the time
   - c. liked to do things the same way all the time

3. After Dickens became a success, he _____.
   - a. continued to work hard
   - b. stopped writing
   - c. decided to travel and enjoy life

◆ REMEMBERING DETAILS

Reread the passage and fill in the blanks.

1. Dickens left school at _____ to become a reporter.

2. Dickens's first big publishing success was _____.

3. Dickens earned a lot of money from his books and from his reading _____.

4. Dickens traveled throughout Europe and _____.

5. Dickens had _____ children with his wife.

6. Dickens divided his page into _____.

7. Dickens _____ things three times for luck.

◆ MAKING INFERENCES

Circle *T* if the sentence is true and *F* if it is false. Then, underline one sentence in the passage that supports your answer.

	True	False
1. Dickens wanted to be like his father.	T	F
2. Dickens wrote about different types of people.	T	F
3. Because of Dickens's stories, poor people's lives got better.	T	F

◆ TELL THE STORY

Work with a partner. Tell the story of Charles Dickens to your partner. Use your own words. Your partner can ask you questions about the story. Then, your partner tells you the story and you ask questions.

DISCUSSION

Discuss the answers to these questions with your classmates.

1. Are you sloppy or meticulous? Explain.
2. Are people in your country superstitious? What are some of the things people in your country believe in?
3. If you did not have radio or television, what would you do for fun?

WRITING

On a separate piece of paper, write six sentences or a short paragraph. Some people care a lot about the way they look. Some people don't. How do you like to look and dress?

Example: *I don't like to be showy. I like to wear simple clothes.*

UNIT 4

ALFRED NOBEL
(1833–1896)

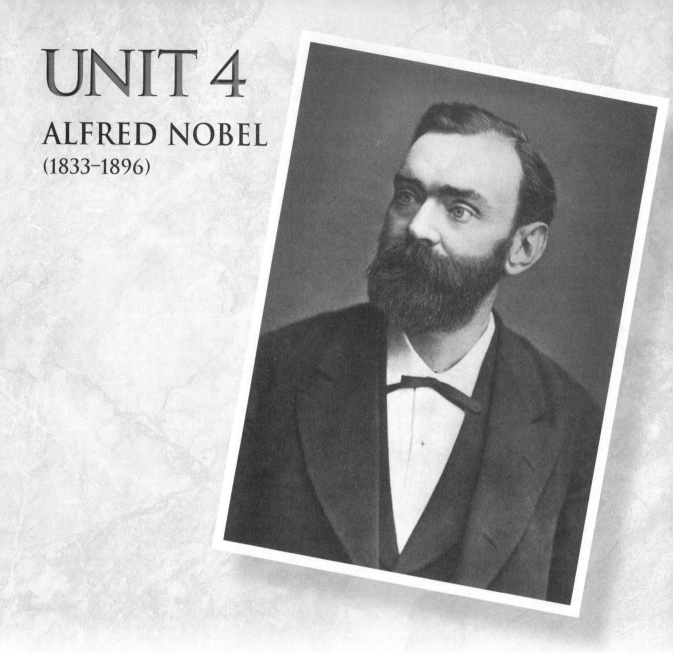

BEFORE YOU READ

Alfred Nobel was a wealthy and successful scientist and inventor. He is most famous for creating the Nobel Prize.

Discuss these questions with a partner.

1. Who has won a Nobel Prize?
2. Who do you think should win a Nobel Prize for science?
3. Who do you think should win a Nobel Prize for world peace?

Now read about Alfred Nobel.

ALFRED NOBEL

The Nobel Prize is one of the greatest honors in the world today. Once a year, people win this prize for their work in science, medicine, literature, economics, or world peace. Each winner receives a gold medal, a diploma, and about $1 million. They also earn the respect of people around the world.

Nobel Prize winners receive their awards at ceremonies in Stockholm, Sweden, and Oslo, Norway, on December 10, the anniversary of the death of Alfred Nobel. Nobel was a scientist and inventor. In his will, he left his fortune to create the Nobel Prize. Nobel wanted people to remember him as a man of peace, but in his lifetime he was most famous for building **weapons** of war.

Alfred Nobel was born in 1833 in Stockholm, Sweden. His father, Immanuel, was an inventor. After Alfred was born, his father went to Russia to work. He worked with the government and made machinery and **explosives.** Several years later, Immanuel moved his family to Russia. Alfred and his two older brothers were interested in science and enjoyed watching their father in the laboratory.

When Alfred was 17 years old, he traveled to the United States and several European countries to study. Then he returned to Russia to work with his father and his brothers. They worked on explosive weapons for the Russian military. At that time, the military used only one type of explosive—gunpowder. Then a chemistry professor showed the Nobels a heavy, oily liquid they could use in their work. It was called nitroglycerin. Nitroglycerin was a powerful explosive, but it was dangerous to work with.

Alfred and his father experimented with nitroglycerin. Finally, in 1863, Alfred invented a way to make it more safe. Scientists everywhere praised his work. Nitroglycerin had many good uses. Workers used it to build roads through mountains and to construct mines deep in the earth.

Nobel's invention was not perfect, however. Nitroglycerin exploded if someone dropped it or used it incorrectly. Sometimes it leaked from the cans. Sometimes workers used the oily liquid on wheels or to clean their shoes! This often caused accidents and injuries. After a while, some governments started to **ban** nitroglycerin because it was dangerous.

The Nobels continued to experiment to make nitroglycerin safer. Unfortunately, in September 1864, Alfred's brother, Emil, was killed in an explosion in their laboratory. After the accident, Immanuel had a **stroke** and was **paralyzed.** He died eight years later, on the same day Emil had died.

Alfred Nobel wanted to make nitroglycerin safe. He built a new laboratory and continued his work. In 1867, he discovered a new material to mix with the nitroglycerin. This material made the nitroglycerin safer and more **effective.** He called his new invention "dynamite."

Nobel built factories all over the world. He continued his experiments and developed new and more powerful explosives. He also became interested in weapons. He developed a new type of gunpowder as well as other materials. Nobel became very wealthy. Many people said he was a bad person because he invented **destructive** weapons. But he believed that nations would stop wars if they had weapons that could destroy each other.

In 1888, Alfred Nobel's older brother, Ludwig, died. A newspaper story confused him with Alfred and called him "the

merchant of death." This upset Alfred very much. He wanted people to remember him as a man of peace. Seven years later he wrote out his will and created the Nobel Prize. When he died in 1896, people called his will the greatest gift ever made by one person. Since 1901, men and women from around the world have received Nobel Prizes for their great achievements. People everywhere now remember Alfred Nobel for his efforts to make the world a better and more peaceful place.

VOCABULARY

◆ MEANING

Match the words with their meanings.

___ 1. merchant	a. something used to fight with
___ 2. weapon	b. damage to the brain that causes loss of movement in parts of the body
___ 3. stroke	c. person who buys and sells goods
___ 4. ban	d. materials used to blow up things
___ 5. paralyzed	e. not able to move
___ 6. explosives	f. able to destroy something
___ 7. destructive	g. producing the result you want
___ 8. effective	h. to stop, or not allow

◆ USE

Work with a partner and answer these questions. Use complete sentences.

1. What are *explosives* used for?
2. What are some modern *weapons*?
3. What are some things that are *banned*?
4. What things are hard for *paralyzed* people to do?
5. What are some things that are *destructive*?
6. What is the most *effective* way to learn new vocabulary?

COMPREHENSION

◆ UNDERSTANDING THE READING

Circle the letter of the best answer.

1. The Nobel brothers _____.
   a. all had different careers
   b. worked with their father
   c. didn't like their work

2. During Alfred Nobel's lifetime, many people _____.
   a. won the Nobel Prize
   b. didn't like his inventions
   c. received money from him

3. Alfred Nobel created the Nobel Prize because _____.
   a. he wanted people to remember him in a good way
   b. he wanted to honor his father
   c. he wanted people to know he had a lot of money

◆ REMEMBERING DETAILS

Reread the passage and fill in the blanks.

1. Each winner of the Nobel Prize receives _____ , _____ , and _____.

2. Alfred's father went to work in _____ and then moved his family there.

3. Before Alfred went to work with his father and brothers, he went to _____ and _____.

4. In 1864, Emil Nobel died in an explosion in their _____.

5. When Alfred Nobel discovered a way to make nitroglycerin safe, he called his new invention _____.

6. Men and women around the world have received Nobel Prizes since _____.

◆ MAKING INFERENCES

Circle _T_ if the sentence is true and _F_ if it is false. Then, underline one sentence in the passage that supports your answer.

	True	False
1. Alfred Nobel's inventions were used only by the military.	T	F
2. Alfred Nobel didn't care about other people's opinions of him.	T	F
3. Alfred Nobel didn't work after Emil's death.	T	F

Work with a partner. Tell the story of Alfred Nobel to your partner. Use your own words. Your partner can ask you questions about the story. Then, your partner tells you the story and you ask questions.

DISCUSSION

Discuss the answers to these questions with your classmates.

1. What are some other ways to honor people who have done important things?
2. Nobel Prizes are given for science, medicine, literature, economics, and world peace. If you could add another category, what would it be?
3. Should the government let people carry guns?

WRITING

On a separate piece of paper, write six sentences or a short paragraph. Describe something that is dangerous.

Example: *The air in my hometown, Tokyo, is dangerous. There is a lot of pollution.*

UNIT 5
SOFIA KOVALEVSKY
(1850–1891)

BEFORE YOU READ

Sofia Kovalevsky was the first woman mathematics professor in Sweden and the first woman to win the famous mathematics prize, the Prix Bordin.

Discuss these questions with a partner.

1. Who are some famous women in history?
2. What were they famous for?
3. What famous woman do you admire?

Now read about Sofia Kovalevsky.

SOFIA KOVALEVSKY

In the 1800s, women could not go to college and have professions. Women who became doctors, scientists, and businesswomen had to **overcome** great **obstacles.** Many of these women went against laws, traditions, and the wishes of their families. However, they **were dedicated to** their work and made great contributions to the world. Sofia Kovalevsky was one of these women.

Sofia was born in 1850 in Moscow. Her father was a Russian general. Her mother was the daughter of a well-known mathematician. The family lived in a large mansion near St. Petersburg. Each of them lived in a separate part of the mansion. Her parents were very strict. Sofia didn't think her parents loved her. She remembered this all of her life.

Sofia loved mathematics at a very early age. When she was 11 years old, she hung up notes from mathematical lectures on her walls. She also taught herself physics. A family friend thought Sofia should study mathematics in St. Petersburg. Sofia's father agreed. When she was 15 years old, she went there with her mother and sister.

Sofia and her sister wanted to go to school, but Russian universities didn't admit women and their father wouldn't let them study **abroad.** Sofia's sister thought of a plan. They needed to find a student to marry one of them. The sisters didn't care which one of them got married. They also didn't care who they found. A student named Vladimir Kovalevsky agreed to their plan. He promised to take his new wife to study in Germany. There was one problem. He liked Sofia, but Sofia didn't care about him.

Their father refused to allow the marriage. At that time, younger sisters never married before their older sisters. But Sofia wanted to go to school very much. So, she left a note for her father and went to Kovalevsky's apartment. At that time, a young woman never spent time alone with a young man. Her father had to agree to the marriage to save the family's honor.

The Kovalevskys went to Germany, and Sofia became a mathematics student. They lived apart and rarely saw each other. Sofia was very lonely and studied all of the time. In 1871, she moved to Berlin to work with a famous mathematician. Women were not allowed to attend the University of Berlin. The mathematician was very surprised when she asked him to teach her. He gave her some problems that even his advanced students could not solve. When Sofia solved the problems, he accepted her as his student immediately. Three years later, Sofia Kovalevsky received her degree in mathematics.

During these years, Sofia Kovalevsky worked completely alone. She had no social life. Vladimir, her husband, also lived in Berlin, but they lived apart. After five years of friendship, however, they finally fell in love. In 1878, they had a daughter. Kovalevsky stopped studying. She wanted to be a good wife and mother. At last she had love and happiness.

Vladimir taught at the University of Moscow. After a while, he left his teaching job. He began to have money and job problems. Sadly, he lost all of their money and then **committed suicide.** Sofia was **devastated.**

A great Swedish mathematician helped Kovalevsky get a job as a mathematics professor in Sweden. She became famous because she was the only woman to be a professor in Europe, outside of Italy. In 1888, Kovalevsky **competed** for the greatest mathematics prize of her time, the Prix Bordin. She worked on a problem about the rings around the planet Saturn. When the Paris Academy of Sciences announced the winner, everyone was amazed that it was a woman. They gave Kovalevsky twice the usual prize money, because she had **solved** a problem that was very important to science.

In 1890, Sofia Kovalevsky became the first woman elected to the St. Petersburg Imperial Academy of Science. Unfortunately, her life and brilliant career ended early. In December 1890, she caught a cold. She got very sick, and she died on February 10, 1891, at the age of 41.

VOCABULARY

◆ MEANING

What is the best meaning of the underlined words? Circle the letter of the correct answer.

1. Sofia's father didn't want her to study <u>abroad</u>.
   a. at a university   b. alone   c. in another country

2. Sofia <u>was dedicated to</u> her work.
   a. worked very hard at   b. changed her mind about   c. showed no fear of

3. Sofia <u>solved</u> an important problem.
   a. found an answer to   b. worked a long time on   c. thought about

4. Vladimir <u>committed suicide</u>.
   a. killed himself   b. ran away   c. went to jail

5. Women like Sofia had to <u>overcome</u> many problems.
   a. find the answer to something   b. think about something carefully   c. fight against something and win

6. Sofia was <u>devastated</u> about what happened to her husband.
   a. unable to understand   b. very sad and upset   c. worried

7. In the nineteenth century, there were many <u>obstacles</u> for women.
   a. ideas about education   b. things that made it hard to succeed   c. ways to get around

8. Sofia <u>competed</u> for the Prix Bordin.
   a. tried to win   b. finished   c. gave the correct answers

◆ USE

Work with a partner and answer these questions. Use complete sentences.

1. What *obstacles* must you *overcome* to find happiness or success?
2. Where would you like to travel *abroad*?
3. When do people *compete*?
4. What people, ideas, or work *are* you *dedicated to* in your life?
5. How do people feel when they are *devastated*?
6. When people have problems in their lives, what should they do to *solve* them?

COMPREHENSION

◆ UNDERSTANDING THE READING

Circle the letter of the best answer.

1. When Sofia was a young girl, she _____ .
   a. refused to live by society's rules
   b. tried to please her father
   c. didn't have the courage to be different

2. Sofia's father believed in _____ .
   a. modern ideas
   b. tradition
   c. doing what was best for Sofia

3. The most important thing to Sofia was to _____ .
   a. make a lot of money
   b. marry a man she loved
   c. succeed in her career

◆ REMEMBERING DETAILS

Reread the passage and answer the questions.

1. What subject did Sofia teach herself?
2. Where did Sofia go to study mathematics at age 15?
3. Where did Vladimir Kovalevsky promise to take Sofia?
4. Why did the Paris Academy of Sciences give Sofia twice the usual prize money?
5. Why was Sofia well known after she became a mathematics professor in Sweden?

◆ MAKING INFERENCES

Circle *T* if the sentence is true and *F* if it is false. Then, underline one sentence in the passage that supports your answer.

	True	False
1. Sofia never loved Vladimir.	T	F
2. Vladimir was very successful.	T	F
3. Sofia was afraid to do things by herself.	T	F

◆ TELL THE STORY

Work with a partner. Tell the story of Sofia Kovalevsky to your partner. Use your own words. Your partner can ask you questions about the story. Then, your partner tells you the story and you ask questions.

DISCUSSION

Discuss the answers to these questions with your classmates.

1. If you wanted a special career and your family was against it, what would you do?
2. Would you marry a person that you didn't love? Why or why not?
3. What are some things that are still difficult for women today?

WRITING

On a separate piece of paper, write six sentences or a short paragraph. Write about a subject you are interested in, and explain why.

Example: *I love art. I like to paint and draw people.*

UNIT 6

VINCENT VAN GOGH
(1853–1890)

BEFORE YOU READ

Vincent van Gogh was one of the first great modern artists. However, during his life, people did not understand him or his work, so he lived and died poor and unhappy.

Discuss these questions with a partner.

1. What famous artists do you know?
2. Do you prefer a painting with nature, people, or something else?
3. Look at the picture of Vincent van Gogh. What can you say about him?

Now read about Vincent van Gogh.

VINCENT VAN GOGH

Today, a painting by Vincent van Gogh sells for more than $80 million. But while he was alive, no one wanted to buy his work. Most people either ignored him or laughed at him.

Vincent van Gogh was born in 1853 in Groot-Zundert, Holland. His father was a church minister. He taught Vincent that it was important to help others. Van Gogh tried to be a minister too, but he was not successful. He tried many other jobs also. He worked as an art seller, a bookseller, and a teacher. He failed at each one. Unfortunately, van Gogh had **mental** problems and was often sad or angry. This made it difficult for him to succeed.

Van Gogh was very good at one thing—art. He taught himself to draw and paint. Van Gogh drew all the time. He drew on anything he could find—menus, books, and **scraps** of paper. In 1881, he began to study art, first in Brussels, then in Paris. His early paintings were about poor people in Holland. They were dark pictures and the people in them were sad. When he went to France, he started to paint with bright colors. He painted in an exciting way, and his paintings showed his strong feelings. He always painted the ordinary things in life—his bedroom, a chair, or some flowers. Often he went into **the country** to paint birds, flowers, and fields.

Van Gogh's paintings were very different from the paintings of other artists, and people didn't like them. Sometimes he left his paintings when he moved to a different place. When people found the paintings, they used them for firewood or to build things. He couldn't sell his work, so he didn't have much money. He often did not have food to eat because he used his money to buy paints and brushes. He also gave clothes and food to other poor people.

Van Gogh's mental problems made his life very difficult. He had a strange, **moody** personality. He was **stubborn** and liked to argue. Some people were afraid of him. Others laughed at him. Children threw things at him in the street and called him bad names. His brother Theo was his only real friend. Theo was an art seller. He believed that Vincent was a genius. Theo gave him money and **encouraged** him to keep working.

Van Gogh spent the last two years of his life in southern France. During this time, he created almost 200 paintings. In 1888, French artist Paul Gaugin went to live with van Gogh. One night they had a terrible argument. Van Gogh **chased** Gaugin down a street with a razor. Later van Gogh was very sorry. He went home and cut off a piece of his left ear. He lost so much blood that he almost died.

Van Gogh realized that he needed help. He went to a mental hospital. While he was there, he continued to paint. In fact, in the last 70 days of his life, he painted a picture every day. He painted one of his best works, *Starry Night,* while he was looking out from his bedroom window at the hospital. Van Gogh went in and out of mental hospitals for many months. Finally, on July 27, 1890, he shot himself. He died two days later. He was only 37 years old.

Theo was full of **sorrow** over his brother's death. He became sick and died only six months later. He was just 33 years old. Theo's widow, Johanna, worked hard to make van Gogh and his paintings well known. Less than 30 years after his death, van Gogh was called one of the greatest artists of all time.

VOCABULARY

◆ MEANING

Write the correct words in the blanks.

encourage	chase	mental	moody
the country	sorrow	stubborn	scrap

1. _____ is a feeling of great unhappiness, especially over the loss of someone or something.

2. Some people have _____ problems. They have problems with their minds.

3. When you _____ people, you support them and tell them to go on with something.

4. A _____ person is someone whose feelings change often and quickly.

5. A small piece of something, such as paper or cloth, which is left over but which can still be used is a _____ of something.

6. The area that is outside of cities or towns is _____.

7. People who are _____ won't change their minds no matter what anyone says.

8. To _____ is to run after someone or something in order to catch it.

◆ USE

Work with a partner and answer these questions. Use complete sentences.

1. Why are *moody* people difficult to be with?
2. How do people often show their *sorrow*?
3. What kinds of things can you do to *encourage* someone?
4. What animals *chase* each other?
5. When is it good to be *stubborn*?
6. Would you rather live in *the country* or in the city?

COMPREHENSION

◆ UNDERSTANDING THE READING

Circle the letter of the best answer.

1. Vincent van Gogh decided to be an artist _____.
   a. when he finished   b. because his father   c. after he failed
      art school   wanted him to   in all his other jobs

2. Van Gogh cared _____.
   a. only about himself   b. about nobody   c. about other people

3. When no one wanted to buy van Gogh's work, _____.
   a. he continued to paint   b. his brother told him   c. he gave up his art
                                   to stop painting   and got other jobs

◆ REMEMBERING DETAILS

Reread the passage and answer the questions.

1. When did van Gogh begin to study art?
2. Where did van Gogh go to study art?
3. What subjects did van Gogh like to paint?
4. Who helped van Gogh in his career?
5. What part of his body did van Gogh cut off?
6. How many paintings did van Gogh paint during the last two years of his life?
7. When did people finally realize that van Gogh was a great artist?

◆ MAKING INFERENCES

Circle *T* if the sentence is true and *F* if it is false. Then, underline a sentence in the passage that supports your answer.

	True	False
1. Van Gogh tried to paint like the other artists of his time.	T	F
2. Theo was right about Vincent's abilities.	T	F
3. Van Gogh was a very happy person.	T	F

◆ TELL THE STORY

Work with a partner. Tell the story of Vincent van Gogh to your partner. Use your own words. Your partner can ask you questions about the story. Then, your partner tells you the story and you ask questions.

Discussion

Discuss the answers to these questions with your classmates.

1. Vincent van Gogh said, "One becomes a painter by painting." He thought that talent wasn't important. Do you agree with him? Give your reasons.
2. Are all creative people a little bit different? Can they have ordinary lives? Give examples.
3. There are many different types of painting. What type of painting do you like?

Writing

On a separate piece of paper, write six sentences or a short paragraph. Describe someone who you care about and that you are always there for.

Example: *I am very close to my sister. I help her when she has problems.*

UNIT 7

MAGGIE WALKER
(1867–1934)

BEFORE YOU READ

Maggie Walker was the first woman bank president in the United States. She grew up poor, but she became a successful businesswoman.

Discuss these questions with a partner.

1. What job would you like to have?
2. Why do you want to have this job?
3. What do you need to do to get it?

Now read about Maggie Walker.

MAGGIE WALKER

Maggie Walker was born in 1867 in Richmond, Virginia. Her mother was once a **slave** in a rich woman's house. When Maggie was very young, a thief killed her father. Her family was poor, so Maggie's mother started doing laundry in her home. Maggie had to help her. She washed clothes every day, but she continued to go to school. She was a very good student, especially in math.

After Maggie graduated from high school, she got a job as a teacher. In 1886, she married Armistead Walker. They had two sons and Maggie stayed home to care for them. She also volunteered to help a social organization called the Order of St. Luke. This organization helped African Americans take care of the sick and bury the dead. Maggie Walker loved the work of the organization. The organization believed that African Americans should take care of each other.

Over the years, Maggie Walker had more and more responsibilities with the organization. In 1895, she suggested that St. Luke begin a program for young people. This program became very popular with schoolchildren. In 1899, Walker became Grand Secretary Treasurer of the St. Luke organization. However, because she was a woman, she received less than half the salary of the man who had the job before her.

The Order of St. Luke had a lot of **financial** difficulties when Walker took over. It had a lot of unpaid bills and only $31.61 in the bank. But soon Maggie Walker changed all of that. Her idea was to get new **members** to join the organization. In just a few years, it grew from 3,400 members to 50,000 members. The organization bought a $100,000 office building and increased its **staff** to 55. Now Walker was ready for her next big step.

In 1903, Walker decided the organization needed its own bank. So she helped to establish the St. Luke Penny Savings Bank. Maggie Walker became its president—she was the first woman to be a bank president in the United States. The bank was very important for African Americans. It gave loans to families so they could buy their own homes. The bank also encouraged children to save money. They could save small amounts of money in a little box the bank gave them. Then they could open a savings account with only $1. But Walker's hard work and generosity also helped white people. Other banks wouldn't give the city schools more money. St. Luke's gave them a loan and saved the school system. The bank still exists today under the name Consolidated Bank and Trust Company.

Walker was not only a businesswoman. She always found time to help her **community.** She published a newspaper called the *St. Luke Herald,* raised money for a girls' school, started a visiting nurse service for the poor and sick, and helped to build a hospital. In 1907, Walker fell and was never able to walk again. She was in a wheelchair for the rest of her life. But she continued her work at the newspaper and the bank for almost 30 more years.

In 1915, something terrible happened in the Walker house. Maggie's son shot her husband, Armistead, by mistake because he thought Armistead was a thief. There was a trial, and Walker supported her son all the time. Luckily, he did not go to prison.

In 1932, Maggie Walker retired from the bank. She died two years later. Her funeral was one of the largest in the history of Richmond. The city named a high school, a theater, and a street after her. The Walkers' home is now a national historic **site.**

VOCABULARY

◆ MEANING

Write the correct words in the blanks.

financial	staff	slave	community
site	loans	establish	members

1. The people who belonged to the St. Luke organization were its

   _____.

2. The organization didn't have much money. Maggie Walker helped to fix their _____ problems.

3. Walker liked to help the people who lived in Richmond. She did a lot for the

   _____.

4. Walker was very important in African American history. That is why her house is a historic _____.

5. The people who worked at the bank were its _____.

6. Many years ago, a rich family owned Maggie's mother. She had no freedom. She was a _____.

7. The bank gave families _____ to help them buy houses. The families used the money, then paid the money back at a later time.

8. Walker helped to _____ the St. Luke Penny Savings Bank. She helped start the business.

◆ USE

Work with a partner and answer these questions. Use complete sentences.

1. What group or organization have you been a *member* of?
2. Where is your *community* located?
3. What business would you *establish* if you had the chance?
4. What is a famous historic *site* in your country?
5. Where can people get *financial* help?
6. What is the name of a member of the *staff* at your school?

COMPREHENSION

◆ UNDERSTANDING THE READING

Circle the letter of the best answer.

1. Maggie Walker had great success because _____.
   a. her family helped her   b. she worked very hard   c. she was a woman

2. Walker helped St. Luke's with its money problems by _____.
   a. getting more members   b. finding more volunteers   c. getting a bigger staff

3. Walker always wanted _____.
   a. the power of money   b. to help other people   c. to keep people and business separate

◆ REMEMBERING DETAILS

Reread the passage and answer the questions.

1. What job did Walker have after she graduated from high school?
2. At first, what did the Order of St. Luke do to help African Americans?
3. Why did Walker receive less money for being Grand Secretary Treasurer than the person who had the job before her?
4. How many members did St. Luke's have when Walker took over?
5. How much money did children need to open a savings account at the bank?
6. What did the community do for Walker after she died?

◆ MAKING INFERENCES

Circle _T_ if the sentence is true and _F_ if it is false. Then, underline one sentence in the passage that supports your answer.

	True	False
1. After Walker became rich, she didn't have any problems.	T	F
2. Walker's ideas changed St. Luke's future.	T	F
3. The St. Luke Penny Savings Bank was good for everyone in the community.	T	F

◆ TELL THE STORY

Work with a partner. Tell the story of Maggie Walker to your partner. Use your own words. Your partner can ask you questions about the story. Then, your partner tells you the story and you ask questions.

DISCUSSION

Discuss the answers to these questions with your classmates.

1. Would you volunteer for an organization? Why or why not?
2. What kinds of things would help your community be a better place to live?
3. Banks today use more and more computers and fewer people. Banks in Maggie Walker's time were very different. Which do you prefer and why?

WRITING

On a separate piece of paper, write six sentences or a short paragraph. Describe the perfect job for you. Give reasons for your choice.

Example: *The perfect job for me is to be a nurse because I like to help sick people.*

UNIT 8

HELENA RUBINSTEIN
(1870–1965)

BEFORE YOU READ

Helena Rubinstein started the world-famous cosmetics company that is named after her.

Discuss these questions with a partner.

1. What are some of the most successful cosmetics companies today?
2. What kind of products do they sell most?
3. What products are popular today that were not popular 50 years ago?

Now read about Helena Rubinstein.

HELENA RUBINSTEIN

In 1950, Helena Rubinstein was one of the richest women in the world. She started with nothing. She had no money, no education, and no one to help her. All she had were 12 jars of face cream and a lot of energy and ambition. She turned these into a multimillion-dollar cosmetics **empire.**

Helena Rubinstein was born in 1870 in Krakow, Poland. She was the oldest of eight girls. Helena's mother thought that beauty was very important. She used a special skin cream that a Hungarian chemist made for her. Helena's mother made all of her daughters use it too.

Helena's father wanted her to be a doctor. But she hated medicine and left school. Her father was very angry. Then he wanted her to get married, but she refused. In 1902, she went to Melbourne, Australia, to live with a cousin and an uncle. She took only her clothes and 12 jars of the face cream.

Helena didn't speak English. She had no money and no plans. After she arrived, everyone noticed her beautiful skin. In Australia the hot, dry weather is very bad for the skin. When she told some of the women about the face cream, they all wanted some. Helena sold them her cream and then ordered more.

Helena borrowed $1,500 and opened a shop to sell the cream. She worked 18 hours a day, seven days a week. She lived simply and saved all of her **profits.** She also learned how to make different kinds of creams and showed women how to take care of their skin. It was the first shop of this kind in the world.

In less than two years, Rubinstein had paid back her loan and saved $50,000. She made more and more money every year.

All this time, she thought only of work and success. A newspaper reporter named Edward Titus was in love with her. But she was not interested in him. She left Australia and went to Europe to learn more about the science of beauty.

In 1908, Rubinstein decided to open a shop in London. Everyone told her she was crazy because English women didn't use beauty products. But she didn't listen. Her shop was a big success. Meanwhile, Titus went to London and **convinced** her to marry him. In 1909, they had a son. Two years later, she moved her family to Paris and opened another shop. In 1912, they had another son.

Helena Rubinstein wasn't a very good wife or mother. Her work was the most important thing to her, and she dreamed only of **expanding** her business. She wanted everyone to be like her, especially the people who worked for her. She paid them very little money and they worked very hard. But Rubinstein was never satisfied. She always thought they should do more.

In 1915, Rubinstein moved her family to the United States. She wanted to open a shop in New York City. Again, people told her it was foolish. At that time, respectable American women didn't wear lipstick or makeup. Again, Rubinstein knew better. By 1917, she had seven shops in the United States and one in Canada. In addition, thousands of shops and department stores sold her products. She was a great success. People called her "the beauty queen." Strangely, she never followed her own beauty advice because she never had time!

Rubinstein was a **workaholic.** She never stopped working, and she **ignored** her family. Her husband once told her,

"Nothing will ever change you, Helena. Your business is your life." They divorced in 1930.

Helena Rubinstein was a **ruthless** businesswoman. Her money gave her great power. She used it to buy **possessions** and people. In 1938, she married Prince Gourielli. He was 20 years younger than she was, and he had no money or power. But he was a prince and she liked that very much. When he died in 1956, she didn't even return from her vacation for his funeral. "He's dead," she said. "Why waste the money?"

Rubinstein was very strange about money. She spent thousands of dollars on travel, jewelry, and art. But she also ate lunch at her desk because it was cheaper than going out. She argued with taxi drivers about how much to pay them. She used the stairs instead of the elevator to save electricity. And she never retired. Rubinstein continued working until she died at the age of 94.

VOCABULARY

◆ MEANING

Match the words with their meanings.

____ 1. expand	a. to not pay attention to someone or something
____ 2. profits	b. very cruel and without caring
____ 3. possessions	c. money you make when you sell something for more than you paid for it
____ 4. convince	d. large group of businesses controlled by one person or company
____ 5. ruthless	e. to become larger
____ 6. ignore	f. things that a person owns
____ 7. workaholic	g. to make someone believe in something or do something
____ 8. empire	h. someone who works all the time

◆ USE

Work with a partner and answer these questions. Use complete sentences.

1. What are some ways to *convince* someone to agree with you?
2. What are your most valuable *possessions*?
3. What are some ways to *expand* a business?
4. How do you think *workaholics* spend their vacations?
5. What are some things that a *ruthless* businessperson does?
6. Do you ever *ignore* people?

COMPREHENSION

◆ UNDERSTANDING THE READING

Circle the letter of the best answer.

1. Helena Rubinstein opened her first shop because _____.
   a. her father wanted her to start her own company
   b. people wanted her face cream
   c. she had to pay back her loan

2. Rubinstein felt that success was _____.
   a. the most important thing in her life
   b. not very important
   c. easy

3. One of the reasons for Rubinstein's huge success was that _____.
   a. she had a good education
   b. she was the first person to open up beauty shops
   c. many people liked her and helped her

◆ REMEMBERING DETAILS

Reread the passage and fill in the blanks.

1. Helena's father wanted her to study to be a _____.

2. Helena left her family in _____ and went to live in _____.

3. Rubinstein sold her _____ to Australian women.

4. The first two European cities where Rubinstein opened new shops were _____ and _____.

5. After Rubinstein became successful, people called her _____.

6. Rubinstein married Gourielli because he was a _____.

7. Rubinstein worked until she was _____.

◆ MAKING INFERENCES

Circle *T* if the sentence is true and *F* if it is false. Then, underline one sentence in the passage that supports your answer.

	True	False
1. As a young woman, Rubinstein tried to please others.	T	F
2. Rubinstein was very good to her workers.	T	F
3. Rubinstein cared more about money than about people.	T	F

◆ TELL THE STORY

Work with a partner. Tell the story of Helena Rubinstein to your partner. Use your own words. Your partner can ask you questions about the story. Then, your partner tells you the story and you ask questions.

Discussion

Discuss the answers to these questions with your classmates.

1. Are there countries where women use more beauty products than others? Why is this so?
2. Helena Rubinstein cared more about her business than about people. Is this the reason she was successful in business? Why or why not?
3. We think of cosmetics as something only for women. Do men use cosmetics or other beauty products? Did they use them in the past? Will they use them in the future?

Writing

On a separate piece of paper, write six sentences or a short paragraph. Describe the most important thing in a person's life.

Example: *The most important things in my mother's life are her children.*

UNIT 9

JULIA MORGAN
(1872–1957)

BEFORE YOU READ

Julia Morgan was one of America's first female architects. She designed many beautiful and famous buildings throughout the United States.

Discuss these questions with a partner.

1. What is a beautiful and famous building in your city?
2. What is special about it?
3. What are some famous buildings around the world?

Now read about Julia Morgan.

JULIA MORGAN

In 1919, a very rich American named William Randolph Hearst wanted to build a new house. Most rich people lived in mansions, but Hearst wanted something bigger and more elegant. He wanted a **castle**. He hired **architect** Julia Morgan to design it for him. Hearst Castle in San Simeon, California, is now one of the most famous buildings in the world. This **extravagant** house has 58 bedrooms, 61 bathrooms, a theater, and a zoo! Morgan worked on it for more than 20 years. Hearst Castle is her most famous work, but she also built more than 800 other buildings. Her great talent and success helped other women to become architects.

Julia Morgan was born in 1872 to a wealthy family in San Francisco, California. She had one sister and three brothers. Julia was a small, weak child, but her mother encouraged her to work hard. She studied hard and did very well in school. After she finished high school, Julia went to the University of California at Berkeley. In those days, few women went to college. In fact, Julia was often the only woman in her math and science classes. In 1894, she became the first woman to graduate from the university with a degree in **civil engineering**.

One of Julia's teachers was an architect named Bernard Maybeck. After graduation, Julia went to work as his assistant. He encouraged her to apply to the École des Beaux-Arts in Paris. The École was the most famous art school in the world at that time. In 1896, Julia left for Paris to study for the entrance exams.

In Paris, Julia Morgan worked for a French architect for two years. She practiced drawing and designing. She also learned to speak and write in French. Morgan failed the entrance exams two times but she was not **discouraged**. Most students failed them at least twice. On her third try, she passed. She was the first woman to attend the École des Beaux-Arts, but she was not allowed to sit with her classmates. She had to sit behind a screen in all her classes because she was a woman. In 1902, Morgan became the first woman to graduate from the École's department of architecture.

Morgan returned to California and became the first woman to receive an architect's license. In 1904, she opened her own architectural office. Morgan was talented and soon had a lot of work. Her most important project during this time was rebuilding the Fairmont Hotel in San Francisco. An earthquake in 1906 had destroyed it. After Morgan completed the Fairmont, she had so much work that she hired assistants to help her. She tried to hire women whenever possible. She also gave money to several schools to help female architecture students.

In 1915, William Randolph Hearst hired Morgan to design a Los Angeles office building. Four years later, he asked her to build the castle. Hearst was very **demanding**. He wrote Morgan hundreds of letters full of instructions, and he often changed his mind. Sometimes he told her to build something, then he told her to take it down and rebuild it in another place. In the end, he sometimes asked her to rebuild it a third time in its original place! Morgan's work was meticulous. She paid careful attention to Hearst's requests and wasn't afraid of hard work. She wore pants under her skirt and climbed ladders to check the work herself. For more than

20 years she traveled 200 miles from San Francisco to San Simeon three weekends a month. For all of her work over so many years, Morgan received only $70,000.

Morgan never married. She was always busy with her work, so she didn't have time for other interests or much of a social life. Her only social life was to visit her mother and her married sister. Morgan had surgery that left her face **crooked** and also **affected** the way she spoke and moved. But she still continued to design schools, churches, public buildings and private homes.

In 1946, at age 78, Julia Morgan closed her office and traveled for the rest of her life. She died in 1957 at the age of 85. Her buildings still influence architects today.

VOCABULARY

◆ MEANING

Write the correct words in the blanks.

demanding	castle	discouraged	extravagant
crooked	affected	architect	civil engineering

1. The good news really _____ her. Her life was much better now.

2. When people lose the desire or spirit to do something, they are

   _____.

3. The king lived in a big, beautiful _____.

4. A person who is _____ wants a lot of time and attention from others.

5. Something that is _____ costs too much money.

6. When something is not straight, it is _____.

7. _____ is the planning, building, and repair of large buildings, roads, and bridges.

8. An _____ is a person who designs new buildings and makes sure they are built correctly.

◆ USE

Work with a partner and answer these questions. Use complete sentences.

1. Who are the most *demanding* people in your life?
2. What *affects* your sleep?
3. What is the most *extravagant* thing you own?
4. Where can you see *castles*?
5. When do some people become *discouraged*?
6. What kinds of jobs do people who study *civil engineering* have?

COMPREHENSION

◆ UNDERSTANDING THE READING

Circle the letter of the best answer.

1. Julia Morgan's business was very successful because she _____.
   - a. was a woman
   - b. had a lot of talent and worked hard
   - c. knew rich people who gave her a lot of money

2. William Randolph Hearst was rich and _____.
   - a. difficult to work with
   - b. very generous
   - c. very helpful

3. After Morgan had surgery, she _____.
   - a. continued to work for a while
   - b. closed her office right away
   - c. finished Hearst Castle, then closed her office

◆ REMEMBERING DETAILS

Reread the passage and fill in the blanks.

1. Hearst Castle is in _____.

2. Often, Morgan was the only woman in her _____ and _____ classes.

3. Morgan failed the _____ twice before she attended the École.

4. When Morgan returned to California, she became the first woman to receive an _____.

5. Morgan's first job for William Randolph Hearst was to design an _____.

6. It took Morgan over _____ years to design and build Hearst Castle.

7. After Morgan closed her office at age 78, she _____.

◆ MAKING INFERENCES

Circle *T* if the sentence is true and *F* if it is false. Then, underline one sentence in the passage that supports your answer.

	True	False
1. Morgan had a lot of work because of her family connections.	T	F
2. Architecture was the most important thing in Morgan's life.	T	F
3. Morgan was treated like all the other students at the École des Beaux-Arts.	T	F

◆ TELL THE STORY

Work with a partner. Tell the story of Julia Morgan to your partner. Use your own words. Your partner can ask you questions about the story. Then, your partner tells you the story and you ask questions.

DISCUSSION

Discuss the answers to these questions with your classmates.

1. Julia Morgan did not get married or have much of a social life. Do most successful people have to give up these things?
2. Describe an extravagant house you have seen. What was special about it?
3. If you could design any type of house for yourself, what would it look like?

WRITING

On a separate piece of paper, write six sentences or a short paragraph. Describe a beautiful house or building.

Example: *In New York City I saw a beautiful hotel. Its name was the Plaza Hotel.*

UNIT 10

PRINCESS KA'IULANI
(1875–1899)

Tynan Bros./Courtesy of Bishop Museum

BEFORE YOU READ

Princess Ka'iulani was a Hawaiian princess. She had great courage and tried to stop the United States government from taking control of Hawaii.

Discuss these questions with a partner.

1. Where are the Hawaiian Islands and what is the weather like there?
2. What do you know about the people and places in Hawaii?
3. Look at the picture of Princess Ka'iulani. What can you say about her?

Now read about Princess Ka'iulani.

PRINCESS KA'IULANI

On October 16, 1875, a child was born in Hawaii. Her name was Victoria Ka'iulani. Ka'iulani was a princess because her uncle, King Kalakaua, did not have children. So the people of Hawaii were very happy when Ka'iulani was born. Ka'iulani's childhood was like a **fairy tale**. The little princess played with giant turtles and fed beautiful birds on her island home. She rode a white horse and went surfing and swimming. She was a sweet, happy child, and everyone loved her.

Ka'iulani's fairy tale ended when she was only 11 years old. Her mother, Princess Likelike, suddenly became very ill. The day Likelike died, she told her daughter, "You will go far away from your land and your people. You will never marry and you will never be queen of Hawaii."

Ka'iulani was very sad after her mother's death. She was then second in line to be queen after her aunt, Liliuokalani. Ka'iulani needed to prepare to be queen. She had to learn about the world around her. When she was 14 years old, she went to England to study. Ka'iulani was afraid to leave her home, but she had to. It was her royal **duty**. Her father sailed with her to San Francisco. Then she took a train to New York and another ship across the Atlantic Ocean. It was a long and difficult journey.

Ka'iulani went to a private girls' school in England. She made friends easily and loved to study. She was very happy there, but she missed Hawaii. She wrote cheerful letters to her family and friends. But the letters from home gave her more and more bad news.

For many years, other countries wanted to control the Hawaiian Islands. Hawaii was a perfect place for **ports** and military bases. When Ka'iulani left Hawaii, her country was already in danger. A group of American businessmen were telling King Kalakaua what to do. Many of them were the sons of religious **missionaries**. These missionaries had gone to the islands in the 1800s to teach Hawaiians about Christianity. They wanted the Hawaiians to learn a new religion, culture, language, and government. Over the years their families had become rich and powerful. They often treated the Hawaiians badly. Eventually, these men controlled the government and all the important businesses. In 1891, they forced King Kalakaua to give up some of his powers. They wanted Hawaii to be under American control. They wanted to **annex** Hawaii to the United States.

King Kalakaua tried to stop the Americans. But he died suddenly and his sister, Liliuokalani, became queen. She was stronger than her brother, and she did not listen to the Americans. They could not control her, so they forced her to give up her power. Then they established their own government.

Ka'iulani was devastated when she heard this news. She wanted to help her people, but she didn't know what to do. She decided to talk to the President of the United States, Grover Cleveland. Ka'iulani was only 17 years old. She was afraid, but she had to try to save her country.

Ka'iulani went to the United States and met the President. While she was there, she made many speeches. She wanted the American people to help Hawaii. People respected her for her courage and **dignity**. President Cleveland asked Congress to allow Liliuokalani to be queen again. But the Americans in Hawaii refused to give up their new government. In 1897, Congress voted to annex Hawaii. The Hawaiians were angry and sad, but they couldn't do anything. They were now a **minority** in their own country because so many other people had moved there.

Ka'iulani went home to be with her people. She tried to bring them peace and happiness, but it was impossible. At age 23, Ka'iulani became very ill. She was full of **despair** and was too weak to fight her illness. On March 6, 1899, Ka'iulani died. As her mother told her, she traveled far, she never married, and she never became queen of Hawaii.

VOCABULARY

◆ MEANING

Write the correct words in the blanks.

annex	fairy tale	duty	dignity
missionaries	despair	ports	minority

1. _____ go to different countries to teach about their religion.

2. In Hawaii, there are many good _____ where boats can load and unload things.

3. By the late 1800s, there were not as many Hawaiians as there were white and Asian people in the Hawaiian Islands. The Hawaiians were a _____ in their own country.

4. When people are very sad and don't have hope, they feel _____.

5. Ka'iulani didn't want the United States to _____ Hawaii. She didn't want the United States to take control of her country.

6. Ka'iulani was a good and serious person. She had great _____ .

7. Her childhood was like a happy story where magic things happened. It was like a _____.

8. As a princess, Ka'iulani had to do what was right and required. She had to do her _____.

◆ USE

Work with a partner and answer these questions. Use complete sentences.

1. As a child, what were some of your favorite *fairy tales*?
2. What are some cities that have famous *ports*?
3. What group of people are a *minority* in your country?
4. When do people feel *despair*?
5. What are some of the *duties* that ordinary people have in their lives?
6. Do *missionaries* still travel around the world? What countries do they go to?

COMPREHENSION

◆ UNDERSTANDING THE READING

Circle the letter of the best answer.

1. Ka'iulani's mother told her daughter _____.
   a. about the future   b. that the United States   c. that she didn't want
                             would annex Hawaii   her to become queen

2. After King Kalakaua died, Ka'iulani _____.
   a. became the queen   b. couldn't save   c. wasn't interested
                             her country   in Hawaii's future

3. The American businessmen wanted to _____.
   a. keep their power   b. educate the Hawaiians   c. help Hawaiians keep
                                                         their own government

◆ REMEMBERING DETAILS

Reread the passage and answer the questions.

1. Why was Ka'iulani a princess?
2. Where did Ka'iulani go to study?
3. Where did her father sail to with her?
4. Why did other countries want to control the Hawaiian Islands?
5. When did Congress vote to annex Hawaii?
6. Who did Ka'iulani talk to when she went to America to ask for her country's freedom?

◆ MAKING INFERENCES

Circle *T* if the sentence is true and *F* if it is false. Then, underline one sentence in the passage that supports your answer.

	True	False
1. Princess Ka'iulani didn't love her mother, Princess Likelike.	T	F
2. If the Americans didn't annex Hawaii, another country probably would have.	T	F
3. Ka'iulani was very sad at the end of her life.	T	F

◆ TELL THE STORY

Work with a partner. Tell the story of Princess Ka'iulani to your partner. Use your own words. Your partner can ask you questions about the story. Then, your partner tells you the story and you ask questions.

DISCUSSION

Discuss the answers to these questions with your classmates.

1. Is the life of a king, queen, prince, or princess better than the life of an ordinary person? Why?
2. Would you like to live on an island? Why or why not?
3. Do you think some people know what will happen in the future?

WRITING

On a separate piece of paper, write six sentences or a short paragraph. Describe a royal person (king, queen, prince, or princess).

Example: *Diana Spencer ws very young when she married Prince Charles. Her life changed a lot after they got married.*

UNIT 11

ISADORA DUNCAN
(1878–1927)

BEFORE YOU READ

Isadora Duncan was a famous dancer. People all over the world loved her unique style of dancing.

Discuss these questions with a partner.

1. What famous dancers do you know? What kind of dancing do they do?
2. What dances have been popular for a long time? What dances have been popular for just a short time?
3. Look at the picture of Isadora Duncan. What can you say about her?

Now read about Isadora Duncan.

ISADORA DUNCAN

Isadora Duncan always wanted to be different. She loved to dance, but she didn't like traditional dances. She refused to learn classical ballet. Instead, Isadora listened to the music and moved naturally. She walked, jumped, or just stood **still** and moved from side to side. No one had ever danced like that before. She was the creator of modern dance.

Isadora Duncan was born in 1878 in San Francisco, California. She was the youngest of four children. Her parents got divorced soon after Isadora was born. Isadora's mother, Dora, always told her children that marriage was terrible. Isadora believed her and promised never to marry. Dora was a music teacher. She earned very little money, so the family was poor. They often couldn't pay the rent, so they moved from place to place. Dora believed that children should be free, so Isadora grew up with few rules. Dora also encouraged Isadora to dance and to love the **arts**.

At age 6, Isadora began to teach other children to dance. By age 10, she was so successful that she decided to quit school. She said school was a waste of time. Isadora had little **formal** education, but she taught herself a lot. She read books by all the great writers and studied the arts.

At age 16, Isadora tried to become a professional dancer. She couldn't find a job because nobody liked her style of dancing. She went from city to city, year after year. Everyone turned her away, but she tried very hard. When she was 18 years old, she got a small part in a play in New York City. She stayed there for a while, then she decided she wanted to go to London. Isadora didn't have much money, so some of her friends gave her money. Life in London was very difficult at first. But after a while, people noticed her. They liked her unique way of dancing. Rich people asked her to dance at their parties. As the years went by, Duncan became famous and danced in all the great cities of Europe. Her lifestyle became famous too. She shocked everyone. She had two children by two different men from two different countries. She didn't marry either of them.

Isadora Duncan adored her children. Unfortunately, in 1913 something horrible happened. Her children and their nurse were riding in a car in Paris. The car went out of control and rolled into the Seine River. All three of them **drowned**. Duncan was devastated. Her pain never went away.

Duncan opened several dance schools around Europe. All of them failed. She was a great dancer and millions of people admired her. But she wasn't a good businesswoman. She was only interested in her art. Sometimes she refused work because she didn't want to dance just for money. She decided things quickly and emotionally, so she made many bad decisions. Once, a group of Russians offered to open a school for her in Moscow, so she sold everything and went to Russia. When she got there, they changed their minds.

At age 44, Duncan broke her promise to her mother and got married. Her husband was Russian poet Sergei Yesenin, and he was 17 years younger than she was. The marriage was a terrible mistake. Yesenin had mental problems and a very **bad temper**. He threw chairs through windows and broke furniture and doors. Almost every day, he **threatened** to kill Duncan. During this time the couple was traveling a lot because Duncan was performing throughout Europe. When they got to Paris, Yesenin took all their money and went back to Russia. A year later, he committed suicide.

In 1927, Isadora Duncan moved to Nice, France. She was almost 50 years old and had very little money. But she never lost her energy and her love for life. One day she asked a car salesman for a ride in a sports car. She was dressed in a **loose** dress with a long scarf. She got into the car, waved to her friends, and said, "Good-bye, my friends, I am going to my **glory**." When the car started, her six-foot-long scarf got caught in the back wheel. The scarf tightened and broke her neck. Isadora Duncan died instantly.

VOCABULARY

◆ MEANING

Write the correct words in the blanks.

loose	bad temper	still	threatened
glory	arts	formal	drowned

1. Isadora Duncan's clothes were not tight. They were _____.

2. Isadora did not like to study science. She liked the _____—subjects like music, history, language, and literature.

3. Sergei told Isadora that he was going to hurt her or make trouble. He _____ her.

4. Duncan became famous and danced all over the world. She was very happy about all the great things she did. These were her days of _____.

5. Sergei could not control his anger. He had a _____.

6. The children _____ because they were under water for too long.

7. Sometimes Duncan did not move when she danced. She stood _____.

8. Isadora quit school and learned things in her own way. She did not receive a traditional, or _____, education.

◆ USE

Work with a partner and answer these questions. Use complete sentences.

1. What is your favorite subject in the *arts*?
2. What do people wear to a *formal* dinner?
3. What was a moment of *glory* in your life?
4. Why do many people prefer to wear *loose* clothes?
5. What kinds of things does someone do when he or she has a *bad temper*?
6. What would you do if someone *threatened* to hurt you?

COMPREHENSION

◆ UNDERSTANDING THE READING

Circle the letter of the best answer.

1. Isadora Duncan was famous because she _____.
   a. opened many   b. created a new   c. was the best ballet
      ballet schools   style of dancing   dancer of her time

2. The most important thing for Duncan was _____.
   a. money   b. fame   c. her art

3. Duncan's marriage was _____.
   a. a promise to her mother   b. good for her children   c. a bad decision

◆ REMEMBERING DETAILS

Reread the passage and answer the questions.

1. What did Isadora's mother tell her about marriage?
2. Who drowned in the Seine River in Paris?
3. How old was Duncan when she got married?
4. What nationality was Duncan's husband?
5. Where did Duncan move to at the end of her life?
6. How did Duncan die?

◆ MAKING INFERENCES

Circle *T* if the sentence is true and *F* if it is false. Then, underline one sentence in the passage that supports your answer.

	True	False
1. Duncan had a traditional childhood.	T	F
2. Duncan was only interested in money.	T	F
3. Duncan was sad and depressed when she got older.	T	F

◆ TELL THE STORY

Work with a partner. Tell the story of Isadora Duncan to your partner. Use your own words. Your partner can ask you questions about the story. Then, your partner tells you the story and you ask questions.

DISCUSSION

Discuss the answers to these questions with your classmates.

1. Isadora's mother raised her children to be different from others. Is this good? Why or why not?
2. What other famous people have always been "different"? How do you feel about them?
3. Do you think women should marry younger men? Give your reasons.

WRITING

On a separate piece of paper, write six sentences or a short paragraph. Describe ways that you do things differently from other people.

Example: *I don't send birthday cards to people. I telephone them.*

UNIT 12
DIEGO RIVERA
(1886–1957)

BEFORE YOU READ

Diego Rivera was a famous Mexican artist. He had a great interest in the politics of his country and a strong love for the Mexican people.

Discuss these questions with a partner.

1. Where is Mexico? What is Mexico famous for?
2. Would you like to visit Mexico? Why or why not?
3. Look at the picture of Diego Rivera. What can you say about him?

Now read about Diego Rivera.

DIEGO RIVERA

Diego Rivera was born in 1886 in Guanajuato, Mexico. As a child, he was very intelligent and **curious** about everything. He grew up to be a strong and free-thinking man.

Diego graduated from art school at the head of his class. He left Mexico in 1907 and spent many of the next 14 years in Europe. During this time, he continued to study art. The paintings of European artists, such as Spanish painter Pablo Picasso, had a great **influence** on his work. Rivera was also very interested in politics. When he returned to Mexico in 1921, he wanted his art to be a part of the history of his country.

Mexico was not a **democratic** country at that time. But Rivera wanted Mexico to belong to all the people. He also believed that an artist's **role** was to fight for equality. Rivera thought his duty was to teach ordinary people with pictures. He wanted everyone to see his work, so he decided to paint murals. Murals are large pictures painted on the walls of buildings. His murals showed Mexican history, traditions, and culture.

The government gave Rivera permission to paint a mural on a public school building. It was his first important mural, and it was very popular. Soon other painters in Mexico started painting murals too, and Mexico became the world center for mural painting. Altogether, Rivera painted more than two and a half miles of murals in his life. One painting had 124 parts. It showed Mexico's history. Rivera worked on this painting for more than four years. He did all the work himself and often worked 15 hours a day.

Rivera lived in the United States from 1930 to 1934. He painted public buildings in Detroit and San Francisco. But his mural in New York City caused trouble. Rivera was a communist, and he put the communist leader of Russia, Vladimir Lenin, in the mural. Many Americans were very angry about this. They destroyed the mural, and Rivera left the United States.

Rivera was a very big man. He was over six feet tall and weighed over 300 pounds. He was also a great showman. People paid money just to watch him paint. When he painted, he told stories. Usually they were stories he **made up** about himself. People always wanted to hear more of his stories. Rivera had strong opinions about politics and religion, but people still admired him. He had many friends—especially women. He was married many times.

In 1928, Rivera married for the third time. He married artist Frida Kahlo. She was one of Mexico's greatest painters. Some people said she painted better than he did. Rivera always said Kahlo was the best painter, and Kahlo always said Rivera was the best. They loved each other, but their marriage was **stormy**. They had many fights and separations. They even divorced and remarried. Newspapers always wrote about "Frida and Diego." They lived in Mexico City in two separate houses with a bridge between them. Rivera's house was pink and Kahlo's house was blue. They had breakfast together every day, and then they each went home to work. In the evening, they met again for dinner.

Frida Kahlo was in an accident when she was younger, and she was often in great pain. Many of her paintings showed this. She died at the age of 47. Rivera was very **disturbed** by her death, and people said he **aged** suddenly. But the next year he married again. Two years later, Rivera died at the age of 71.

VOCABULARY

◆ MEANING

What is the best meaning of the underlined words? Circle the letter of the correct answer.

1. Diego Rivera <u>made up</u> stories about himself.
   a. told with much feeling   b. created   c. remembered

2. Mexico was not a <u>democratic</u> country in those days.
   a. government where   b. government with   c. government where
      the people choose   military leaders   everyone shares their wealth
      the leaders

3. The marriage of Frida Kahlo and Diego Rivera was <u>stormy</u>.
   a. long lasting   b. famous   c. full of troubles

4. Pablo Picasso had a great <u>influence</u> on Rivera's work.
   a. effect   b. trust   c. fear

5. Rivera believed his <u>role</u> as an artist was to fight for equality.
   a. duty   b. strong belief   c. way of working

6. As a child, Rivera was <u>curious</u> about everything.
   a. interested in knowing   b. bored by new   c. afraid of strange
      about things   things   things

7. Rivera was very <u>disturbed</u> by Kahlo's death.
   a. nervous   b. surprised   c. upset and worried

8. Rivera suddenly <u>aged</u>.
   a. looked younger   b. became older and   c. got very sick
                            weaker

◆ USE

Work with a partner and answer these questions. Use complete sentences.

1. What is something that *disturbed* you?
2. What are some things that *democratic* countries have in common?
3. What is the *role* of a teacher?
4. Who had an *influence* on you when you were a child?
5. What are the advantages and disadvantages of being *curious*?
6. Why do people sometimes *make up* stories?

COMPREHENSION

◆ UNDERSTANDING THE READING

Circle the letter of the best answer.

1. In his early years, Diego Rivera _____.
   a. never went to art school
   b. had an excellent art education
   c. studied art in the United States

2. Rivera painted murals because _____.
   a. it was a way to show his art to all the Mexican people
   b. he wanted to paint the largest pictures possible
   c. he believed it was a way to make buildings more beautiful

3. People loved Rivera because he _____.
   a. wanted to work in the Mexican government
   b. had a great talent and a strong personality
   c. always lived in Mexico

◆ REMEMBERING DETAILS

Reread the passage and fill in the blanks.

1. When Rivera was studying art, _____ had an influence on his work.

2. In his murals, Rivera showed Mexico's _____, _____,
   and _____.

3. Rivera's huge mural of 124 parts was about _____.

4. Rivera got into trouble in _____ because he painted a mural with a
   communist leader in it.

5. People loved to watch Rivera paint because he told _____ while he
   worked.

6. Rivera and Kahlo lived in Mexico City in _____.

◆ MAKING INFERENCES

**Circle _T_ if the sentence is true and _F_ if it is false. Then, underline one sentence in
the passage that supports your answer.**

	True	False
1. Rivera was interested only in his art.	T	F
2. Everything about Rivera was large: his body, his personality, even his art.	T	F
3. Everyone always loved and accepted Rivera's work.	T	F

◆ TELL THE STORY

Work with a partner. Tell the story of Diego Rivera to your partner. Use your own words. Your partner can ask you questions about the story. Then, your partner tells you the story and you ask questions.

DISCUSSION

Discuss the answers to these questions with your classmates.

1. Do you think two famous people can live happily together? Why or why not?
2. The Americans destroyed Diego Rivera's mural because they didn't agree with the political ideas in it. Was this the right thing to do? Why or why not?
3. If you were married, would you and your husband or wife live in separate houses? Explain.

WRITING

On a separate piece of paper, write six sentences or a short paragraph. Write about a famous painter, singer, dancer, or actor from your country.

Example: *A famous actor from my country, Egypt, is Omar Sharif.*

UNIT 13

JIM THORPE
(1888–1953)

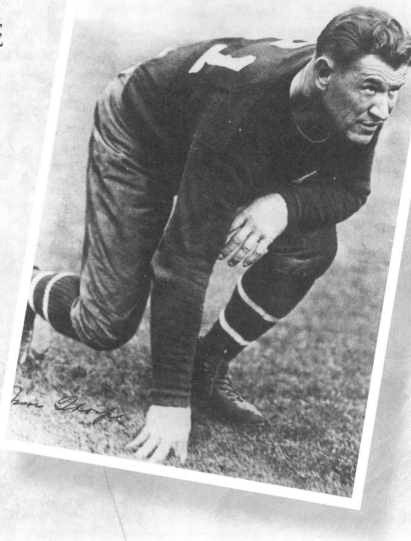

BEFORE YOU READ

Jim Thorpe was one of America's greatest athletes. He won two gold medals at two of the most difficult events in the Olympics.

Discuss these questions with a partner.

1. When and where were the last Olympics?
2. What are some sports events in the Olympics?
3. What sport do you like to watch most in the Olympics?

Now read about Jim Thorpe.

JIM THORPE

In 1950, Jim Thorpe was named the greatest American football player and the best athlete of the first half of the twentieth century. He was also an Olympic gold medal winner and a national hero. But Thorpe had many **tragedies** in his life. Even his greatest **achievements** did not make him rich or happy.

Jim Thorpe was a Native American. He was born in 1888 in an Indian Territory that is now Oklahoma. Like most Native American children then, he liked to fish, hunt, swim, and play games outdoors. He was healthy and strong, but he had very little formal education.

Jim had a twin brother who died when he was nine years old. This was the first tragedy of his life, but not the last. By the time he was 16, his mother and father were also dead. Jim then went to a special school in Pennsylvania for Native American children. There, he learned to read and write and also began to play sports. Jim was poor, so he left school for two years to earn some money. During this time, he played on a baseball team. The team paid him only $15 a week. Soon he returned to school to complete his education. Jim was a star athlete in several sports, including baseball, running, wrestling, and football. He won many awards for his athletic ability, mainly for football. In many games, he scored all or most of the points for his team.

In 1912, when Jim Thorpe was 24 years old, he became part of the U.S. Olympic team. He competed in two very difficult events: the pentathlon and the decathlon. Both require great ability and strength. The pentathlon has five **track and field** events, including the long jump and the 1,500-meter race. The decathlon has ten track and field events, with running, jumping, and throwing contests.

People thought it was impossible for an athlete to compete in both the pentathlon and the decathlon. So everyone was surprised when Thorpe won gold medals in both events. When the King of Sweden presented Thorpe with his two gold medals, he said, "Sir, you are the greatest athlete in the world." Thorpe was a simple and honest man. He just answered, "Thanks, King."

When Thorpe came home he was an American hero. But all the **praise** did not last for very long. Less than a year later, there was another tragedy. A newspaper reporter found out that Thorpe had played baseball for money. People who earn money for playing sports are called professionals. At that time, professionals could not compete in the Olympics. Only **amateurs** were allowed. Officials decided that Thorpe had to return his gold medals. Many people believed this was unfair. But the Olympic Committee took away his medals and removed his name from the record books.

Thorpe was devastated. At first he decided to stop playing sports. But he was an athlete and had few other skills, so he played professional baseball and football. Unfortunately, Thorpe had another great tragedy in his life. His three-year-old son died of the flu. Many people said that Thorpe never got over this loss.

Thorpe was an **outstanding** football player and helped to make football a popular sport in America. In 1929, he retired from football. He had several jobs and also gave speeches on sports and Native American **issues.** Thorpe was very proud of being a Native American. Unfortunately, some people did not treat him fairly because of his race. This made him sad and angry. He also never forgot that the Olympic Committee took away his medals. He believed they had cheated him.

In 1951, Thorpe became sick with cancer. By that time, he had almost no money. Some groups who remembered his Olympic performance **raised money** to help him. Two years later, Thorpe died of a heart attack. He was 64 years old.

Many people tried to get Thorpe's medals back to him. But it never happened during his lifetime. Thirty years after his death, the medals were finally returned. Six of Thorpe's children attended the ceremony. His name was also put back in the 1912 Olympic record books.

VOCABULARY

◆ MEANING

Match the words with their meanings.

___ 1. track and field	a. to ask for and get money from other people
___ 2. amateurs	b. better than others; very good
___ 3. tragedies	c. good words said about someone
___ 4. issues	d. sports that involve running races, jumping, and throwing
___ 5. raise money	e. things one works hard for and does well at
___ 6. achievements	f. terrible and unhappy events
___ 7. outstanding	g. people who do things, such as play sports, for enjoyment and do not get paid
___ 8. praise	h. subjects or problems that people discuss

◆ USE

Work with a partner and answer these questions. Use complete sentences.

1. What is something that you would like to *raise money* for?
2. What is an important *issue* in your country?
3. What *achievements* do you want to have in your lifetime?
4. What *tragedy* have you heard about in the news recently?
5. Who are some of today's *outstanding* athletes?
6. What are some ways to *praise* someone?

COMPREHENSION

◆ UNDERSTANDING THE READING

Circle the letter of the best answer.

1. During his childhood, Jim Thorpe _____.
   a. spent a lot of time studying
   b. had some problems
   c. didn't like sports

2. People were amazed when Thorpe won Olympic gold medals _____.
   a. at such a young age
   b. in two very difficult events
   c. because he was a Native American

3. After Thorpe lost his gold medals, he _____.
   a. wanted to return to the Olympics
   b. was upset about it for the rest of his life
   c. understood why the Committee took away the medals

◆ REMEMBERING DETAILS

Reread the passage and fill in the blanks.

1. As a child, Thorpe developed a strong body because he liked to _____, _____, _____, and play games outside.

2. By the time Jim was _____, his parents had died.

3. In the Olympics of 1912, Thorpe won two _____.

4. _____ later, a reporter found out that Thorpe played baseball for money.

5. When Thorpe worked as a professional athlete, he played _____ and _____.

6. Thorpe's medals were finally returned _____ after his death.

◆ MAKING INFERENCES

Circle *T* if the sentence is true and *F* if it is false. Then, underline one sentence in the passage that supports your answer.

	True	False
1. Thorpe was a natural athlete.	T	F
2. People did not care that Thorpe lost his medals.	T	F
3. Thorpe wanted to help other Native Americans.	T	F

◆ TELL THE STORY

Work with a partner. Tell the story of Jim Thorpe to your partner. Use your own words. Your partner can ask you questions about the story. Then, your partner tells you the story and you ask questions.

DISCUSSION

Discuss the answers to these questions with your classmates.

1. Sometimes there are good reasons an athlete isn't allowed to play, or a medal or honor is taken away. What do you think is a good reason?
2. How are today's Olympics different from those of 1912?
3. Some people say that a person who had a difficult childhood tries harder to succeed than a person who had an easy childhood. Do you agree? Why or why not?

WRITING

On a separate piece of paper, write six sentences or a short paragraph. Describe something you think was not fair.

Example: *I was the best student in art in my school. We had an art contest in my town. I entered, but I did not win. The reason wasn't because I was not a good artist.*

UNIT 14

AGATHA CHRISTIE
(1890–1976)

BEFORE YOU READ

Agatha Christie was a famous mystery writer. Even today, long after her death, she is one of the most popular writers in the world.

Discuss these questions with a partner.

1. What are mystery stories about?
2. What are some famous mystery television shows or movies?
3. Look at the picture of Agatha Christie. What can you say about her?

Now read about Agatha Christie.

AGATHA CHRISTIE

Agatha Christie is often called the "Queen of Crime." But Christie was not a thief or a murderer. She was a very respectable woman. She earned this title because she wrote some of the most popular mysteries and **detective stories** in the world.

Agatha was born in 1890 in Devonshire, England. As a child, she loved to hear and tell stories. Agatha never went to school, but she was very **bright.** She loved books and taught herself to read before she was five years old.

Agatha wrote her first short story when she was 18 years old. Her first **novel,** *The Mysterious Affair at Styles,* was published in 1920. By then, she was married to Archibald Christie. Soon after, she wrote four more popular novels. In 1926, *The Murder of Roger Ackroyd* was published. Some people didn't like it because an unusual character was the murderer. Others called it one of the greatest detective stories of all time. It was the book that made her famous.

Christie was very successful. But her marriage was unhappy. Her husband, Archibald, was in love with a woman named Nancy Neele, and Agatha was devastated. She was also upset because some people didn't like her new book. On December 3, 1926, Agatha Christie did something very mysterious. She got into her car, drove away, and disappeared. Someone found her car the next day. Christie's coat was on the seat and the car lights were on. For ten days, thousands of police officers and volunteers looked for her. The newspapers wrote stories about the real-life mystery of the mystery writer.

On the eleventh day, someone found Christie at a hotel. She was talking with other guests and acting very normal. She said her name was Teresa Neele, the same last name as her husband's lover! Christie never explained her actions, but she and her husband got divorced a short time later. In 1930, she married Max Mallowan. He was an archeologist, a scientist who studies ancient cultures. He was 14 years younger than she was. They were very happy together. Christie once said, "It's wonderful to be married to an archeologist—the older you get, the more interested he is in you."

Christie tried to write a novel for Christmas each year. She wrote for over 50 years and produced a **remarkable** amount of work. She wrote 66 novels, 15 plays, and 157 short stories. Once, one of Christie's books saved someone's life. A little girl was very sick. The doctors tried everything, but she only got worse. One of the girl's nurses was reading Christie's mystery story *The Pale Horse.* In the story, the murderer kills his **victim** with a poison called thallium. The victim's **symptoms** described in the book were like the little girl's symptoms. The nurse thought, "Did this little girl **swallow** thallium?" She told the doctors about the **case.** They tried a new medicine and saved the girl's life.

Agatha Christie liked to write stories about two detectives. Their names were Miss Marple and Hercule Poirot. Miss Marple is a quiet, unmarried woman who lives in a small village. She notices everything that happens. She is very bright and always solves the crimes before the police do. Hercule Poirot is a retired Belgian detective. He has a very good opinion of himself and is very neat and meticulous. Readers loved the characters of Miss Marple and Hercule Poirot and always wanted to read their next cases.

Sometime in the 1940s, Christie wrote the last cases for Miss Marple and Hercule Poirot. Readers wanted more of these stories, so Christie asked for the books to be published after she died. She died on January 12, 1976. Both books became immediate best sellers.

Agatha Christie's books have sold over a billion copies in English and another billion in over 45 other languages. Her books still continue to sell. She is now the most popular British author in the world and the fifth best selling author of all time. That is why some call her the "Queen of Crime."

VOCABULARY

◆ MEANING

What is the best meaning of the underlined words? Circle the letter of the correct answer.

1. Agatha Christie wrote <u>detective stories</u>.
   a. untrue stories about faraway places
   b. love stories with a happy ending
   c. stories where someone tries to solve a crime

2. In a mystery story, there is usually a murderer and a <u>victim</u>.
   a. person who is hurt or killed in a crime
   b. person who helps with a crime
   c. person who sees a crime

3. Agatha was very <u>bright</u> as a child.
   a. intelligent
   b. serious
   c. well mannered

4. Miss Marple always solved the <u>case</u> before the police did.
   a. story that people talk about
   b. money problem
   c. situation that the police investigate

5. Christie produced a <u>remarkable</u> number of stories.
   a. common
   b. unusual
   c. small

6. The victim's <u>symptoms</u> were like the little girl's symptoms.
   a. things that make someone feel better
   b. things that are sad
   c. things that show that someone might be sick

7. The nurse wondered if the girl <u>swallowed</u> thallium.
   a. touched it with her hand
   b. smelled it and breathed it in
   c. put it in her mouth and down her throat

8. Christie wrote a <u>novel</u> for Christmas each year.
   a. story which is not true
   b. true story about a real person
   c. book with short stories

♦ USE

Work with a partner and answer these questions. Use complete sentences.

1. What is your favorite *novel*?
2. Who do you think is a *remarkable* person?
3. What kinds of *cases* do the police work on?
4. What kinds of things do you *swallow* quickly?
5. What do you like or dislike about *detective stories*?
6. What are some *symptoms* you have when you get a cold?

COMPREHENSION

♦ UNDERSTANDING THE READING

Circle the letter of the best answer.

1. When Agatha Christie disappeared, she _____.
   a. was a victim of a crime   b. got a lot of attention   c. didn't want to write anymore

2. Christie's mystery story *The Pale Horse* saved a girl's life because it _____.
   a. was a popular book with doctors and nurses   b. made the police look for the murderer   c. described the symptoms of thallium poisoning

3. Readers like Miss Marple and Hercule Poirot because they _____.
   a. never are able to solve the crimes   b. give them ideas on how to solve crimes   c. are interesting characters

♦ REMEMBERING DETAILS

Reread the passage and fill in the blanks.

1. The book that made Christie famous was _____.
2. After Christie disappeared, someone found her car with the lights on and a _____ on the seat.
3. Christie's second husband worked as an _____.
4. Christie tried to write a least one novel for _____ every year.
5. A girl's life was saved because her _____ was reading *The Pale Horse*.
6. Miss Marple lived in _____.
7. Christie's last two books were published after she _____.

◆ MAKING INFERENCES

Circle *T* if the sentence is true and *F* if it is false. Then, underline one sentence in the passage that supports your answer.

	True	False
1. Readers became bored with Miss Marple and Hercule Poirot.	T	F
2. Miss Marple didn't need special training and scientific methods to solve crimes.	T	F
3. Christie's stories are no longer interesting to today's readers.	T	F

◆ TELL THE STORY

Work with a partner. Tell the story of Agatha Christie to your partner. Use your own words. Your partner can ask you questions about the story. Then, your partner tells you the story and you ask questions.

DISCUSSION

Discuss the answers to these questions with your classmates.

1. Why do you think Agatha Christie disappeared?
2. Do you prefer to see a movie or read a book? Why?
3. Why do some people like detective stories?

WRITING

On a separate piece of paper, write six sentences or a short paragraph. Describe a television show or movie about police or detectives.

Example: *I watch* Murder, She Wrote. *It is about a woman that is a detective.*

UNIT 15

LOUIS ARMSTRONG

(1901–1971)

BEFORE YOU READ

Louis Armstrong was a famous jazz trumpet player. He was born poor. Later in life, he played music for both royalty and ordinary people all over the world.

Discuss these questions with a partner.

1. What is your favorite kind of music?
2. What kinds of music are popular today?
3. Look at the picture of Louis Armstrong. What can you say about him?

Now read about Louis Armstrong.

LOUIS ARMSTRONG

Louis Armstrong was one of the greatest jazz trumpet players in the world. He traveled to many countries and helped to make jazz popular everywhere. Louis was born in 1901 in New Orleans, Louisiana. His family was poor, and his father left when Louis was very young. Louis sang on street corners and worked at small jobs to earn money.

Life got even harder for Louis. On New Year's Eve, 1913, he fired a gun into the air. He did it for fun and nobody was hurt. But the police **arrested** him and put him in a home for problem children. This event changed Louis's life forever. At the home, Louis learned to play the cornet, a musical instrument that is like a trumpet. When he left there 18 months later, he started to play in small jazz bands. Louis Armstrong was so good that the great cornet player Joe "King" Oliver noticed him. Oliver gave Armstrong lessons and helped him learn about the music business.

By age 18, Armstrong quit his other jobs and started to play the cornet full time. In 1922, "King" Oliver asked Armstrong to join him in Chicago. It was a great **opportunity** for Armstrong. Soon Louis Armstrong was more popular than "King" Oliver. For the next few years, Armstrong worked in Chicago, New Orleans, and New York. He played with the most popular musicians of his time. He learned a lot about music. He also began to play the trumpet.

In 1925, Armstrong started his own band called the Hot Five. The band was very successful, and Armstrong became world famous. When he returned to New York in 1929, he was a jazz **idol.**

Armstrong worked very hard in New York. Every evening he was the star in the musical *Hot Chocolate*. After the show, he went to work at a famous nightclub. Soon he was traveling all around the country. He also performed in many Hollywood movies. He often slept too little and ate and drank too much. But he was still strong even when he got older. Armstrong was always **aware of** his health. He was afraid of germs and always carried the mouthpiece of his trumpet in a clean handkerchief in his pocket.

People everywhere loved Armstrong. They loved his warm-hearted personality and his happy smile. They also loved his big, wide mouth. People started to call him "satchelmouth" because his mouth was as big as a large satchel or bag. Then they shortened it to "Satchmo."

Armstrong also became famous for his rough singing voice. He sang more as he got older, because it was harder for him to play the trumpet. He also created a new kind of singing called "scat." In scat, a singer sings **nonsense** syllables instead of words ("ba doo ba dooo ba"). One story says that Armstrong invented it by mistake. One day he dropped his music while he was recording a song. He started to sing nonsense syllables, and scat was born.

People around the world wanted to hear Louis Armstrong. He played for England's King George VI. He toured the Middle East, Asia, and South America. On his world tour in the 1950s, people called him "America's Ambassador of Goodwill." In his 1960 African tour, 100,000 people heard him play in Ghana. But fame and money didn't change Armstrong. He always came back to his **modest** home in a **run-down** neighborhood in New York City. He said he wanted "to be with my people."

After a career of more than 50 years, Louis died in New York City in 1971. He made over 2,000 recordings and more than 30 movies. People everywhere **mourned** his death. In New Orleans, he received a traditional jazz musician's funeral with jazz bands playing and people dancing in the street.

VOCABULARY

◆ MEANING

Write the correct words in the blanks.

opportunity	run-down	aware of	idol
nonsense	modest	mourn	arrest

1. To _____ is to feel very sad, especially when someone dies.

2. Something that is silly or that doesn't have meaning is _____.

3. An _____ is a person or thing that people admire very much.

4. A chance or time to do something is an _____.

5. Something that is _____ is usually old and in bad condition.

6. When police officers catch people who did something against the law, the police _____ them.

7. To be careful about something is to be _____ it.

8. Something _____ is not big and expensive, but simple and low-priced.

◆ USE

Work with a partner and answer these questions. Use complete sentences.

1. What *opportunity* do you want in your life?
2. Who is an *idol* in music today?
3. What are some customs and ceremonies used to *mourn* someone's death?
4. What does a *modest* home in your neighborhood look like?
5. What do you see in a *run-down* neighborhood?
6. What are some of the things that happen when the police *arrest* someone?
7. What do you need to be *aware of* when you write in English?

COMPREHENSION

◆ UNDERSTANDING THE READING

Circle the letter of the best answer.

1. At the home for problem children, Louis Armstrong _____.
    a. met "King" Oliver   b. learned to play music   c. earned money to help his family

2. Joe "King" Oliver gave Louis the chance to _____.
    a. play music in other parts of the country   b. be in movies   c. sing scat music

3. Armstrong was popular because he _____.
    a. was a star in plays and movies   b. could play the cornet   c. had great talent and a good personality

◆ REMEMBERING DETAILS

Reread the passage and answer the questions.

1. Why did the police arrest Louis when he was young?
2. Where did "King" Oliver ask Louis to join him?
3. When did Armstrong start his own band?
4. What musical was Armstrong a star in?
5. Why did people call Armstrong "satchelmouth"?
6. Who did Armstrong play for in England?
7. How many recordings did Armstrong make?

◆ MAKING INFERENCES

Circle _T_ if the sentence is true and _F_ if it is false. Then, underline one sentence in the passage that supports your answer.

	True	False
1. It was bad for Louis to be in the home for problem children.	T	F
2. Joe "King" Oliver helped to change Armstrong's life.	T	F
3. Armstrong was popular only in the United States.	T	F

◆ TELL THE STORY

Work with a partner. Tell the story of Louis Armstrong to your partner. Use your own words. Your partner can ask you questions about the story. Then, your partner tells you the story and you ask questions.

DISCUSSION

Discuss the answers to these questions with your classmates.

1. Do you like jazz? Why or why not?
2. Do fame and money change most people? How do they change?
3. When Louis Armstrong died, there was dancing and jazz music at his funeral. What do you think of this?

WRITING

On a separate piece of paper, write six sentences or a short paragraph. Write about a famous musician or singer.

Example: *Madonna is my favorite singer. I like her because she sings all different types of songs.*

UNIT 16

UMM KULTHUM

(1904–1975)

BEFORE YOU READ

Umm Kulthum was one of Egypt's greatest singers. When she sang, the Arab world listened.

Discuss these questions with a partner.

1. What are some countries in the Arab world?
2. What is the main religion?
3. Who are some famous people from the Arab world?

Now read about Umm Kulthum.

UMM KULTHUM

People called Umm Kulthum "the voice of Egypt." She was born in 1904 in a small village in Egypt. She came from a poor family. Her father was the *imam,* or prayer leader at the local **mosque.** To earn extra money, he sang religious songs for weddings and other celebrations.

Umm's father taught his son to sing, so they could sing together at the celebrations. Umm listened to them and soon learned the songs **by heart.** One day her father heard her singing. He decided to teach Umm too. Once when her brother got sick, Umm sang in his place. Her voice was **exceptionally** strong and clear. Everybody listened in silence. They thought her voice was a gift from God. Soon Umm became the star singer. But no one knew that Umm was a girl. She dressed as a boy because her father thought it was wrong for a girl to sing in public.

Umm and her father began to earn a lot of money. They traveled to other villages so Umm could perform. People said that they should go to Cairo because Cairo was the center for the music business. At first, the family did not want to go because they knew no one in the big city. Finally, in 1923, they decided to move.

In the beginning, Umm Kulthum sang the religious songs she learned from her father. But people said that this kind of music was old-fashioned. So she decided to compete with the other famous singers of the time. She hired teachers, took lessons, and practiced. Then she started to sing modern love songs. She also dressed in elegant clothes and held a long silk handkerchief. This handkerchief became her **trademark.** Kulthum's career really started when she began to make records. By 1928, she was the most popular professional singer in Cairo.

By 1934, radio and movies began to come to Cairo. Kulthum was popular in both. She **broadcast** a **live** concert on the first Thursday of every month. People called it "Umm Kulthum Night." When she sang on the radio, people said that life in the Arab world came to a stop. In 1935, she began to work on the first of six films.

Kulthum chose her songs carefully. Some were popular songs, others were from classical Arab pieces. Her songs connected the people of her country to their history. That is why they called her "the voice of Egypt." Kulthum always sang from her heart. She did not even let her musicians learn to read music because she wanted the music to come from their hearts.

People always wanted to know about Kulthum's personal life. But her **privacy** was important to her. Once one of the king's uncles proposed marriage to her. However, the royal family did not agree to the marriage, and she was deeply hurt. Soon after, she married one of her musicians, but the marriage only lasted a few days. Finally, in 1954, she married Hasan al-Hifnawi, who was one of her doctors. This marriage was successful.

Kulthum had several health problems, but she continued to sing into her seventies. Her concerts always started late in the evening and lasted from three to six hours. During her last concert in December 1972, she felt **faint** but finished the concert anyway. Kulthum planned to sing again but never did. She died in 1975. Four million people filled the streets of Cairo at her funeral. More people came to her funeral than to the funeral of President Nasser! Even today millions of people in the Arab world listen to the songs of Umm Kulthum.

VOCABULARY

◆ MEANING

What is the best meaning of the underlined words? Circle the letter of the correct answer.

1. Umm Kulthum's singing was <u>exceptionally</u> beautiful.
   a. not very   b. unusually   c. only

2. Every month, Kulthum <u>broadcast</u> a concert.
   a. sent out a radio or   b. listened to a radio or   c. recorded a radio or
      television program   television program   television program

3. As a child, Umm learned the songs <u>by heart</u>.
   a. from memory   b. from books   c. by writing them

4. Kulthum gave a <u>live</u> concert on the first Thursday of every month.
   a. recorded   b. very long   c. performed for people
      in advance   who are watching

5. Kulthum's <u>privacy</u> was important to her.
   a. having a lot of   b. not sharing her   c. telling people
      people around her   personal life   about her music

6. Kulthum's father was the *imam* at a <u>mosque</u>.
   a. building where   b. home for poor families   c. place for weddings
      Muslims worship   and celebrations

7. Kulthum felt <u>faint</u> during her last concert.
   a. sad and upset   b. weak and about to   c. sick to her stomach
                            fall down

8. A silk handkerchief was Kulthum's <u>trademark</u>.
   a. special name for   b. something she gave   c. special object that
      her show   to other people   made people think of her

◆ USE

Work with a partner and answer these questions. Use complete sentences.

1. What are the *trademarks* of some popular people or products today?
2. What *live* broadcasts have you heard?
3. What helps us to learn things *by heart*?
4. How do people feel when they feel *faint*?
5. Who are some singers famous for their *exceptionally* good voices?
6. Why is it difficult for famous people to have *privacy*?

COMPREHENSION

◆ UNDERSTANDING THE READING

Circle the letter of the best answer.

1. Umm Kulthum's father felt that _____.
   a. Umm was too young to sing in public
   b. Umm's brother had a better singing voice
   c. Umm had a very good singing voice

2. Kulthum became really popular when she _____.
   a. decided to sing religious songs
   b. didn't compete with other singers
   c. started recording modern love songs

3. Kulthum was so well loved because she _____.
   a. sang for all the Arab people
   b. wore beautiful clothes
   c. gave long concerts

◆ REMEMBERING DETAILS

Reread the passage and answer the questions.

1. Why did Kulthum's father sing at weddings?
2. What kind of songs did Kulthum sing at first?
3. When did Kulthum broadcast her live concerts?
4. What was her trademark?
5. How many times was Kulthum married?
6. How many people came to her funeral?

◆ MAKING INFERENCES

Circle *T* if the sentence is true and *F* if it is false. Then, underline one sentence in the passage that supports your answer.

	True	False
1. Kulthum's father was the only person to help her with her singing.	T	F
2. Kulthum's success helped her family.	T	F
3. Kulthum made a mistake when she began to make records.	T	F

◆ TELL THE STORY

Work with a partner. Tell the story of Umm Kulthum to your partner. Use your own words. Your partner can ask you questions about the story. Then, your partner tells you the story and you ask questions.

DISCUSSION

Discuss the answers to these questions with your classmates.

1. Do you think famous people should have privacy?
2. What are the trademarks of some famous people?
3. Are there any television shows or special events on television that everyone stops to watch?

WRITING

On a separate sheet of paper, write six sentences or a paragraph. Describe the traditional music of your country.

Example: *The traditional music in my country, Mexico, is mariachi music.*

UNIT 17

HOWARD HUGHES

(1905–1976)

BEFORE YOU READ

Howard Hughes was one of the wealthiest and most powerful men of his time. He was famous for his fast and exciting life.

Discuss these questions with a partner.

1. What is your idea of an exciting life?
2. Who is a famous person that has an exciting life?
3. Who is a person that you know that has an exciting life?

Now read about Howard Hughes.

HOWARD HUGHES

People say that money cannot buy happiness. This was true for Howard Hughes. He was one of the richest and most powerful men of his time. He had everything: good looks, **charm**, success, power, and a lot of money. But he didn't have love or friendship because he couldn't buy them. All his life he used his money to control everything and everyone around him. In the end, he lost control of everything, even himself.

Howard Hughes was born in 1905 in Houston, Texas. His father started the Hughes Tool Company. He was a workaholic and made a lot of money. He bought everything he wanted. He even gave money to schools so Howard could get into them. From his father, Howard learned to be a successful but ruthless businessman. Hughes's mother, Allene, also had a big influence on his life. Howard was her only child. She protected him and gave him everything. Unfortunately, Allene had mental problems. She was afraid of germs and disease. She was **obsessed** with Howard's health, and he became obsessed with it too.

Allene died when Howard was 16 years old. Two years later his father died. Hughes **inherited** Hughes Tool Company. Then he married Ella Rice. He and Ella moved to Los Angeles, California. It was there that Howard Hughes began to become a **legend**.

Hughes began to **invest** his money in movies. He became an important producer soon after he moved to California. He worked hard, but he also played hard. He became obsessed with power and control. When he couldn't get something legally, he gave money to politicians and businessmen so they would help him. He owned a lot of businesses, including airplane companies,

a movie studio, Las Vegas hotels, gold and silver mines, and radio and television stations. Once he bought a television studio so he could watch movies all night. He also bought a hotel because he wanted to stay in his favorite room for one weekend.

Hughes loved the wild Hollywood life and dated many famous movie stars. Of course, his marriage ended very quickly. He asked every woman to marry him on the first date. Hughes used people for his pleasure and didn't treat them very well, so he had no real friends.

Howard Hughes loved fast cars and airplanes. He was a **daredevil** pilot and **risked** his life many times. He set many flying records, including the fastest flight around the world at the time. Reporters loved to write about the rich, handsome playboy pilot. But Hughes's love of adventure also hurt him. He was in many airplane and car crashes—14 in all. Once he almost died when his plane crashed into a house. Hughes had serious physical and mental problems because of these accidents.

When Hughes couldn't control a situation, he became ill. He had a lot of mental problems. Once in a while, he just ran away. Sometimes he was gone for months. He changed his name and worked at simple jobs for a while. Then he returned home.

Hughes was very **eccentric.** Every day he got worse and worse. He had the same dinner every night: a steak, a baked potato, and 12 peas. Everything always had to be perfect. His tomatoes had to be cut exactly one-quarter inch thick. His sandwiches had to be cut into exact triangles. As Hughes got older, his behavior became even more strange. Once he stayed in the same room for two and a half years. He was afraid of germs too. He hired people just to kill flies. He also covered everything with tissues. Then he wore the empty tissue boxes on his feet! Sometimes he refused to wear clothes or cut his fingernails and hair.

Howard Hughes died on an airplane in 1976. He was on the way to see a doctor. He was very sick from living such a strange life. Sadly, the rich, handsome playboy lost his mind, his health, and his dignity. He loved no one and no one loved him. Howard Hughes had bought everything in his life, except happiness.

VOCABULARY

◆ MEANING

Match the words with their meanings.

___ 1. daredevil ___ 2. invest ___ 3. charm ___ 4. risk ___ 5. legend ___ 6. obsess ___ 7. eccentric ___ 8. inherit	a. special quality people have that makes other people like them b. to receive something from someone after he or she has died c. very famous person d. person who does dangerous things for excitement and fame e. strange and unusual f. to give money to a company in order to get profit later g. to think about something too much h. to put something in danger

◆ USE

Work with a partner and answer these questions. Use complete sentences.

1. What are some of the things that *daredevils* do?
2. Which person in your class has *charm*?
3. What do you think is a good way to *invest* money?
4. What is something that people *inherit*?
5. What are some things that *eccentric* people do?
6. What are some common *risks* that people take in their daily lives?
7. Who is a *legend* in your country?

COMPREHENSION

◆ UNDERSTANDING THE READING

Circle the letter of the best answer.

1. One reason Howard Hughes was famous was that he _____.
   a. had a difficult b. did many dangerous c. was a very generous
      childhood   things   person

2. The most important thing to Hughes was _____.
   a. friendship   b. education   c. money

3. Hughes liked to do _____.
   a. simple things   b. everything his   c. good things for
      in life   own way   other people

◆ REMEMBERING DETAILS

Reread the passage and fill in the blanks.

1. Hughes inherited _____ after his father died.

2. The legend of Howard Hughes began when he moved to _____.

3. Hughes almost died when his _____ into a house.

4. Hughes wanted to stay in his _____, so he bought a hotel.

5. Sometimes Hughes ran away for months at a time. He changed _____

   and worked at _____ before he went home again.

6. Every night, Hughes ate _____, _____, and

   _____.

7. For two and a half years, Hughes lived in the _____.

◆ MAKING INFERENCES

**Circle *T* if the sentence is true and *F* if it is false. Then, underline one sentence in
the passage that supports your answer.**

	True	False
1. Hughes was a normal, ordinary pilot.	T	F
2. Hughes was a lazy person who got all his money from his father.	T	F
3. Many people loved Hughes because he was kind to them.	T	F

◆ TELL THE STORY

**Work with a partner. Tell the story of Howard Hughes to your partner. Use your
own words. Your partner can ask you questions about the story. Then, your
partner tells you the story and you ask questions.**

DISCUSSION

Discuss the answers to these questions with your classmates.

1. How important is money in your life?
2. Why do you think Howard Hughes didn't get help for his mental problems?
3. What do you think of daredevils or people who risk their lives for fun?

WRITING

On a separate piece of paper, write six sentences or a short paragraph. Write about your idea of an exciting life.

Example: *An exciting life for me is to travel a lot.*

UNIT 18

SOICHIRO HONDA
(1906–1991)

BEFORE YOU READ

Soichiro Honda started the Honda Motor Company. The company became one of the world's largest makers of motorcycles and automobiles.

Discuss these questions with a partner.

1. What are some popular cars and motorcycles today?
2. What is your favorite car or motorcycle?
3. Which do you prefer: a car or a motorcycle? Why?

Now read about Soichiro Honda.

SOICHIRO HONDA

Soichiro Honda was born in 1906 in a small village in Japan. It was so small that it didn't even have electricity. His family was poor. Soichiro had eight brothers and sisters. Sadly, five of them died when they were young because they did not have good medical care. When Soichiro was eight years old, he saw his first automobile. He was **amazed** by it. For the next 50 years, he loved machines on wheels.

When he was 15 years old, Soichiro left his village to work at an auto repair shop in Tokyo. It was then that Honda discovered motorcycles. He spent all of his free time fixing and riding motorcycles. He returned to his village six years later to open his own garage. Soon he owned several shops and had over 50 employees.

At the same time, he began to build and race motorcycles and cars. Honda loved to race, and he became one of Japan's most **competitive** drivers. In 1936, his race car crashed while he was driving 100 miles per hour. Half of Honda's face was **crushed,** and he had other serious injuries. It took him a year and a half to recover. After this, his family **begged** him to **give up** racing. He looked for a less dangerous job and finally decided to become a manufacturer.

At first, he manufactured engine parts. The Japanese navy used a lot of his engine parts in World War II. In 1948, after the war, he started the Honda Motor Company. He started the company with only $3,300. He made his first machines from engine parts that the military did not need after the war. These machines were not real motorcycles; they were bicycles with motors. People bought them because they needed a **reliable** form of transportation.

As Honda's business grew, he began to make different types of motorcycles. By 1950, his motorcycles were selling all over Japan. But there were 50 other motorcycle makers in Japan at the time. In 1958, Honda designed a lightweight motorcycle called the Super Cub. It was a huge success and Honda made a lot of money. Two years later, Honda built the world's biggest motorcycle factory in Japan.

By the 1960s, the Super Cub was popular all over Asia. But Honda wanted the motorcycle to be popular all over the world. In Europe, he put his motorcycles in difficult races to show how good they were. In the United States, he tried a different method. He used a magazine **ad** with the words "You Meet the Nicest People on a Honda." It showed ordinary Americans such as students, businessmen, and older people all riding happily on the Honda Super Cub. The ad appeared in many popular magazines.

Readers who had never ridden a motorcycle saw the ad. The ad showed that motorcycles were not just for crazy young people who wore black leather jackets. They were good for other people too. The company sold thousands of motorcycles to new riders. Honda then started to put the ads on television. This was also very successful. For example, he put an ad for his motorcycle on during the Academy Awards program. Millions of people watched that program, and on the next day, sales of the motorcycle went up **tremendously.** By 1968, Honda had sold 1 million motorcycles in the United States.

In 1963, his company started to make cars. In 1972, it produced the Civic; the next year, the Accord; and then in 1978, the Prelude. Soon, the company was one of the world's biggest automobile makers. Honda was also famous for his business style. He believed that workers and bosses should have a close relationship. He also thought it was important to encourage workers to do their best.

In 1973, Soichiro Honda retired as president of his company. He died in 1991. Honda was very important to Japan's recent history. He and many other business leaders helped make Japan into a leading industrial nation.

VOCABULARY

◆ MEANING

Write the correct words in the blanks.

crushed	competitive	amazed	begged
give up	tremendously	reliable	ad

1. Soichiro Honda's parents wanted him to stop racing cars. They wanted him to

   _____ racing.

2. A Honda _____ gave information about the product so people would buy it.

3. Honda always wanted to be more successful than other people. He was very

   _____.

4. People wanted something _____ that they could trust and depend upon.

5. The car pressed down on his body with great force and _____ his bones.

6. Soichiro's parents asked for a favor that was very, very important to them. They _____ him to stop racing cars.

7. The success of the ad was very great. It was _____ successful.

8. Honda was very surprised and full of wonder. He was _____.

◆ USE

Work with a partner and answer these questions. Use complete sentences.

1. Did you ever *give up* something because someone asked you to?
2. What are *competitive* people like?
3. What is your favorite *ad* on television?
4. Who is a *reliable* person in your life?
5. What is something that *amazes* you?
6. What kinds of things can you *crush*?

COMPREHENSION

◆ UNDERSTANDING THE READING

Circle the letter of the best answer.

1. Soichiro Honda _____.
   a. manufactured cars and motorcycles all his life
   b. wasted his time working at an auto repair shop
   c. was poor when he started out, but later became a success

2. Honda's business was _____.
   a. a huge success in the United States only
   b. small in the beginning and then expanded
   c. a huge success from the beginning

3. Honda was very successful because he _____.
   a. had a good education
   b. wasn't afraid to take chances
   c. owned the only motorcycle maker

◆ REMEMBERING DETAILS

Reread the passage and answer the questions.

1. Where did Honda go when he left his village?
2. What happened to Honda's race car in 1936?
3. When did Honda start the Honda Motor Company?
4. What was different about the new motorcycle that Honda designed?
5. What did Honda's ad say?
6. How many motorcycles did Honda sell in the United States by 1968?
7. From 1975 to 1978, what cars did Honda produce?

◆ MAKING INFERENCES

Circle _T_ if the sentence is true and _F_ if it is false. Then, underline one sentence in the passage that supports your answer.

	True	False
1. The Honda Motor Company started as a simple business.	T	F
2. Only one type of person liked Honda's ad for the Super Cub.	T	F
3. Honda treated his workers badly.	T	F

◆ TELL THE STORY

Work with a partner. Tell the story of Soichiro Honda to your partner. Use your own words. Your partner can ask you questions about the story. Then, your partner tells you the story and you ask questions.

DISCUSSION

Discuss the answers to these questions with your classmates.

1. What do you think the car of the future will be like?
2. Which country do you think produces the best cars?
3. Which product or business has very successful ads?

WRITING

On a separate piece of paper, write six sentences or a short paragraph. Describe a form of transportation and how it has changed over the years.

Example: *To fly on an airplane today is cheaper than before.*

UNIT 19

MOTHER TERESA
(1910–1997)

BEFORE YOU READ

Mother Teresa became famous around the world for helping people. She spent her life caring for people who were poor, sick, and dying.

Discuss these questions with a partner.

1. Who are some people or charity organizations that help the poor and sick? What do they do?
2. Did you ever help with a charity? What did you do?
3. Look at the picture of Mother Teresa. What can you say about her?

Now read about Mother Teresa.

MOTHER TERESA

Mother Teresa was a simple **nun.** She never wanted to be famous, but everyone in the world knew who she was. She received many important awards. She traveled around the world to accept them. She asked people for help. Then she gave everything to the poor.

Mother Teresa was born Agnes Gonxha Bojaxhiu in 1910 in what is now Macedonia. She was the youngest of three children. Agnes's father died when she was a child. Her mother made dresses to support the family. Agnes's mother also liked to do charity work, such as visiting the sick. Agnes often went with her, and she enjoyed helping these people. She was a good and religious girl.

Even as a child, Agnes wanted to be a nun. When she was 18 years old, she joined a group of nuns in Darjeeling, India. There, she chose the name Teresa. Then she went to Calcutta to work at St. Mary's School. The school was in a **convent.** Sister Teresa lived in the convent and worked at the school for 20 years. She eventually became the principal. During all those years, Sister Teresa was always **concerned** about how other people lived. The convent had clean buildings and beautiful **lawns.** But outside the convent, the streets were dirty and crowded and full of very poor people.

One day in 1946, Sister Teresa was riding on a train to Darjeeling. She looked out of the window and saw dirty children. They were wearing **rags** and sleeping in doorways. Sick and dying people were lying on **filthy** streets. She loved her work at the school, but she realized that other people needed her help more. At that moment, she believed God sent her a message. She decided to go to work with the poor.

Two years later, Sister Teresa left the convent. First, she went to a hospital to learn to take care of sick people. After three months, she was ready to live with the poor and the sick. One day, she saw a group of poor children and called them to her. She told them she was going to open a school. The school had no roof, no walls, and no chairs. On the first day, only five students came. She used a stick to write lessons in the dirt.

Several months later, Sister Teresa had many students. Everyone in Calcutta knew about her. A friend let her use part of his house for the school. She taught the children language and math. She also taught them how to keep clean and stay healthy. Soon, other nuns came to help her. Sister Teresa was happy that they wanted to join her. But she told them that life with her was not easy. She said that everyone had to wear the same clothes—white cotton saris. She wanted all the nuns to look like the poor people in India.

In 1948, Sister Teresa started her own group of nuns. They were called the Missionaries of Charity. She was their leader, so they called her "Mother" Teresa. The nuns lived in the **slums** with people who were poor, dirty, and sick. It was hard work and the days were long. But many young nuns came from around the world to join Mother Teresa.

One day, Mother Teresa saw an old woman in the street. She took her to a hospital. They refused to help the woman because she was poor. Mother Teresa decided to open a place for the sick and the dying. Later, she started homes for children without families. She also started clinics. Over the years, news of her work spread around the world. Many people sent her **donations** of money. Others came to work with her in India or other places. By 1990, the Missionaries of Charity were working in 400 centers around the world.

Over the years, Mother Teresa received many great awards, such as the Nobel Peace Prize. But she always said her greatest reward was helping people. Her message to the world was, "We can do no great things—only small things with great love." She died in 1997 at the age of 87. The whole world mourned her death.

VOCABULARY

◆ MEANING

Match the words with their meanings.

___ 1. lawn	a. very dirty
___ 2. nun	b. something that you give to help a person or charity
___ 3. slum	c. ground around a house or park that is covered with grass
___ 4. concerned	d. area of a city that is run-down and in bad condition
___ 5. rags	e. worried about
___ 6. convent	f. woman who belongs to a religious group whose members live together
___ 7. filthy	g. old and torn clothing
___ 8. donation	h. place where nuns live and work

◆ USE

Work with a partner and answer these questions. Use complete sentences.

1. When have you given a *donation*? Did you give money or something else?
2. What are you most *concerned* about right now?
3. Where can you see a *lawn*?
4. Why are some streets *filthy*?
5. What kind of people wear *rags*?
6. What are the buildings like in *slums*?

COMPREHENSION

◆ UNDERSTANDING THE READING

Circle the letter of the best answer.

1. Mother Teresa became famous because she _____.
   a. started a hospital   b. was a good teacher   c. lived her life to help others

2. Mother Teresa's first school _____.
   a. was very small   b. wasn't liked by the   c. taught religious subjects only
      and simple   people of Calcutta

3. The nuns who worked with Mother Teresa _____.
   a. had a very hard life   b. wanted to be famous   c. lived like other nuns

◆ REMEMBERING DETAILS

Reread the passage and answer the questions.

1. Which country did Agnes go to when she was 18 years old?
2. How long did Sister Teresa live and work in the convent in Calcutta?
3. Where did Sister Teresa go right after she left the convent?
4. What was the name of the group of nuns Sister Teresa started?
5. What kind of clothes did Mother Teresa and her group of nuns wear?
6. Why did the hospital refuse to help the woman that Mother Teresa brought to them?
7. Which important award did Mother Teresa receive?

◆ MAKING INFERENCES

Circle *T* if the sentence is true and *F* if it is false. Then, underline one sentence in the passage that supports your answer.

	True	False
1. As a child, Agnes only thought about herself.	T	F
2. Sister Teresa needed a lot of money to open up her first school.	T	F
3. Mother Teresa thought that the awards she received were very important.	T	F

◆ TELL THE STORY

Work with a partner. Tell the story of Mother Teresa to your partner. Use your own words. Your partner can ask you questions about the story. Then, your partner tells you the story and you ask questions.

DISCUSSION

Discuss the answers to these questions with your classmates.

1. What are some things you see in the world today that you don't like?
2. What kind of help do you think governments should give to poor people?
3. What do you think about charity organizations? Do you think they are all honest?

WRITING

On a separate piece of paper, write six sentences or a short paragraph. Write about how you have helped someone.

Example: *My friend George works very hard and makes very little money. Last year, he needed to buy a new refrigerator.*

UNIT 20

SONJA HENIE
(1912–1969)

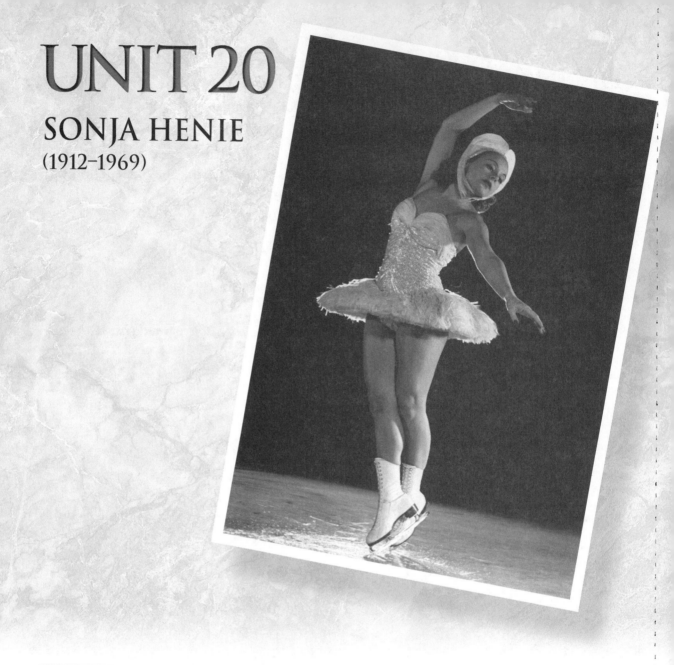

BEFORE YOU READ

Sonja Henie was an Olympic gold medal winner and a world-famous ice skating star. She also became a movie star and was the richest athlete of her time.

Discuss these questions with a partner.

1. Is ice skating popular in your country? Where is ice skating popular?
2. Who are some famous ice skaters?
3. Look at the picture of Sonja Henie. What can you say about her?

Now read about Sonja Henie.

SONJA HENIE

Sonja Henie was born in 1912 in Oslo, Norway. She started to ice skate when she was five years old. At age nine, Sonja won her first skating competition. Her family decided that Sonja should start to **train** seriously. Her father helped her, and she won her first national championship. Sonja was only 11 years old when she **represented** Norway in the Olympics in 1924. She finished in last place, but she got a lot of attention because she was so young. Sonja continued to train. She became a world champion and won a gold medal at the 1928 Olympics. She won two more gold medals in 1932 and 1936. Between 1917 and 1936, Sonja Henie won a total of 1,473 awards.

Henie had a very strong influence on women's figure skating. For example, she **introduced** music and choreography to skating. (Choreography is when you plan your dance to music.) She also introduced **glamour** to skating. Women skaters used to wear long, dark dresses. Henie wore beautiful, short, white costumes.

After she became a professional in 1936, Henie moved to Hollywood. She wanted to be a movie star! She appeared in several movies, and she skated in all of them. The movie company paid her $150,000 a year, which was a lot of money at that time. Sonja Henie was a great success once again.

Everyone wanted to see Henie's movies because they were glamorous and **spectacular.** Henie skated in ice shows also. She went on a world tour with the ice shows, and the performances were always sold out. Her movie fans went to her ice shows and her skating fans went to her movies. When Henie appeared, there was always a crowd. Sonja Henie was a big star.

Henie was also a **tough** businesswoman. She made sure no one cheated her in her movie contracts or her ice shows. She loved money. At age 26, she was a millionaire. She became the richest athlete of her time. Henie married three times. All her husbands were millionaires too.

Henie liked people to know that she was rich. She rode in a white Rolls Royce. She wore white dresses and a lot of jewelry. She lived in a mansion in Hollywood, and she had a chauffeur, a maid, a cook, a secretary, and a hairdresser. She gave big parties and invited all the most famous people to them. For one party, she put a tent over her tennis courts and hired people to fly to Hawaii just to get the best flowers. There were ice carvings everywhere and swans in the swimming pools. She always had the best food and drinks at her parties too.

Henie worked hard for her money. She worked very long hours. When she worked on a film, she got up at five o'clock in the morning, worked for 12 hours, came home, had dinner, and went to bed early. When she was on tour, she stayed up all night and slept half the day. Her **diet** was mainly **raw** eggs and raw beef. She wanted to have a healthy diet, but she ate very few vegetables.

In 1968, Henie and her third husband opened an art center outside of Oslo. This multimillion-dollar center contains most of her awards and her art collection, which is one of the best in the world. Fourteen months after the center opened, Sonja Henie died of cancer at the age of 57.

VOCABULARY

◆ MEANING

Write the correct words in the blanks.

glamour	represent	diet	tough
spectacular	train	introduce	raw

1. To practice a job or activity is to _____.

2. Someone who can deal with difficult things is _____.

3. _____ is a special quality of being beautiful and successful.

4. Something that is not cooked is _____.

5. To _____ is to act officially for someone or something.

6. Something is _____ if it is exciting and unusual.

7. A person's _____ is the kind of food he or she usually eats.

8. To _____ something is to make it happen for the first time.

◆ USE

Work with a partner and answer these questions. Use complete sentences.

1. In which professions do people need to have a lot of *glamour*?
2. What kind of *diet* do you have?
3. In what professions do women have to be *tough*?
4. What is the most *spectacular* thing you have ever seen or experienced?
5. What are some foods that people usually eat *raw*?
6. Have you ever had to *train* for something?

COMPREHENSION

◆ UNDERSTANDING THE READING

Circle the letter of the best answer.

1. Sonja Henie first got attention as a skater because she _____.
   a. created a new style of skating
   b. wore glamorous costumes
   c. was an Olympic skater at a very young age

2. Before Henie came along, ice skaters _____.
   a. were not in the Olympics
   b. dressed and skated in an ordinary way
   c. had to be men

3. Henie lived a full life because she _____.
   a. liked to have all the things money can buy
   b. worked too hard to enjoy her wealth
   c. was wealthy but lived a simple life

◆ REMEMBERING DETAILS

Reread the passage and fill in the blanks.

1. Henie was in the Olympics in 1924 when she was only _____.

2. In 1928, Henie won _____, and in 1932 and 1936, she won

   _____.

3. Women's figure skating changed when Henie wore costumes that were

   _____, _____, and _____.

4. Henie's movies were very popular because they were _____ and

   _____.

5. When Henie worked on a movie, she worked _____.

6. Henie usually ate _____ and _____.

7. Henie rode in a _____ and lived in a _____.

◆ MAKING INFERENCES

Circle *T* if the sentence is true and *F* if it is false. Then, underline one sentence in the passage that supports your answer.

	True	False
1. Henie's skating fans were upset when she became a movie star.	T	F
2. Henie was proud of her wealth.	T	F
3. Henie never worked hard for her money.	T	F

◆ TELL THE STORY

Work with a partner. Tell the story of Sonja Henie to your partner. Use your own words. Your partner can ask you questions about the story. Then, your partner tells you the story and you ask questions.

DISCUSSION

Discuss the answers to these questions with your classmates.

1. If you could see any athlete or movie star perform, who would it be?

2. In many countries, Olympic athletes begin to train at a very young age. Do you think this is a good idea?

3. Do you think Sonja Henie had a healthy diet and lifestyle?

WRITING

On a separate piece of paper, write six sentences or a short paragraph. Write about a spectacular show.

Example: *Last year on New Year's Eve there was a spectacular show in my city.*

UNIT 21

I. M. PEI
(1917–   )

BEFORE YOU READ

I. M. Pei is a world-famous architect. His buildings are everywhere from Hong Kong to Boston. Many of his designs are very unusual.

Discuss these questions with a partner.

1. What is a building that has an unusual design?
2. What is an unusual piece of art?
3. Do you prefer unusual architecture and art or traditional architecture and art?

Now read about I. M. Pei.

I. M. PEI

I. M. Pei is one of the world's greatest architects. People admire his buildings in cities around the world. He is famous for his ability to **combine** old and new architecture.

Ieoh Ming Pei was born in 1917 in Canton, China. He was the oldest son of a wealthy banker. When he was nine years old, his family moved to Shanghai. At that time, Shanghai was a busy city with many new buildings. A 23-story **skyscraper** especially **fascinated** young Ieoh Ming. Over the years, he became more and more interested in architecture.

I. M. Pei received a good education at the best schools in Shanghai. His family lived very well and his childhood was happy. His mother was a talented musician, and Pei was very close to her. Unfortunately, she died when he was only 13 years old.

At that time, many wealthy Chinese families sent their children abroad to college. At the age of 17, Pei went to the United States. He studied engineering and architecture at the Massachusetts Institute of Technology (M.I.T.). He graduated in 1940 and wanted to return to China. But World War II had started, and Pei's father told him it was safer to stay in the United States. During the war, Pei worked for the United States government. His job was to find ways to safely destroy buildings. Pei did not like this work and was very happy when the war ended. After the war, Pei went to the Harvard Graduate School of Design.

Pei planned to return to China after he received his master's degree. But his father said it was dangerous because the communists were **in power.** Again he could not go home. Pei stayed in the United States and worked for a building company in New York City. During this time, he designed homes, office buildings, parks, and shopping centers. Some of these buildings became famous.

In 1955, I. M. Pei started his own company. He designed many buildings for M.I.T. He also designed the Museum of Fine Arts in Boston. He became well known for creating buildings that looked like the things around them. This was very unusual. For example, for a building in the Rocky Mountains, he designed **towers** that looked like the mountains.

Pei was very successful. But one project almost ruined his career. In the early 1970s, his company designed the John Hancock Tower in Boston. The 60-story building was covered with blue-green glass. It looked like a huge mirror. Unfortunately, there was one problem— the windows started to fall out. Over and over, Pei's workers put in new windows. But over and over, they fell out again. Many newspapers in the country had stories about Pei's building. After a while, his company lost a lot of business. Eventually they discovered that the glass was not right. They replaced all of the windows and the problem was solved. Today, people think the John Hancock Tower is one of I. M. Pei's biggest successes.

During this time, Pei went abroad and designed buildings in Kuwait, Singapore, and Hong Kong. In 1974, he visited China for the first time in 40 years. He designed a hotel in Beijing. He also designed the 72-story Bank of China building in Hong Kong. This is one of the tallest buildings in Asia.

One of Pei's most famous works is the National Gallery of Art in Washington, D.C. It was a big **challenge** because he added a new part to an old building. His design was a big success. The president of France saw Pei's work and admired it. He chose Pei to design an addition to the Louvre museum in Paris. Pei added a glass and steel **pyramid** to the 700-year-old building. This was also unusual, because the Louvre is a traditional building and the pyramid is modern. At first, many Parisians were unhappy with the modern addition. But now, many people like his **bold** design.

I. M. Pei is someone who has truly influenced the modern world. He is a great success among architects.

VOCABULARY

◆ MEANING

What is the best meaning of the underlined words? Circle the letter of the correct answer.

1. The communists were <u>in power</u> in China.
   a. in government   b. out of control   c. at war

2. I. M. Pei was interested in a <u>skyscraper</u> in Shanghai.
   a. powerful jet plane   b. place on top of a mountain   c. very tall building

3. It was a <u>challenge</u> for Pei to work on the National Gallery of Art.
   a. something easy to do   b. something hard to do that requires a lot of luck   c. something hard to do that requires a lot of skill

4. The addition to the Louvre in Paris is one of Pei's most <u>bold</u> designs.
   a. simple   b. different   c. well-liked

5. Pei added a <u>pyramid</u> to the building.
   a. modern building   b. triangle-shaped building   c. very big building

6. Pei has the ability to <u>combine</u> old and new architecture.
   a. design   b. put together   c. add to

7. A 23-story skyscraper <u>fascinated</u> young Ieoh Ming.
   a. surprised   b. interested   c. taught

8. The <u>towers</u> looked like mountains.
   a. doors in a building   b. sides of a building   c. tall parts of a building

USE

Work with a partner and answer these questions. Use complete sentences.

1. What political party is *in power* in your country?
2. What do you think has a *bold* design?
3. Where can you see *skyscrapers*?
4. What is your biggest *challenge*?
5. On what kind of building can you see a *tower*?
6. What invention *fascinates* you?

COMPREHENSION

◆ UNDERSTANDING THE READING

Circle the letter of the best answer.

1. When he was a child, I. M. Pei _____.
   a. had a difficult life
   b. didn't have much chance to be successful
   c. had a good start in life

2. In 1940, Pei didn't return to China because _____.
   a. it was dangerous
   b. he didn't have the money for the trip
   c. his family moved to the United States

3. Pei went overseas when he had problems in the United States. This was _____.
   a. very bad for his name
   b. something he did for his father
   c. a good decision

◆ REMEMBERING DETAILS

Reread the passage and fill in the blanks.

1. Pei was born in _____.
2. At M.I.T., Pei studied _____ and _____.
3. During World War II, Pei's job with the government was to _____.
4. On one of his jobs, Pei designed towers that looked like _____.
5. The John Hancock Tower had a problem with its _____.
6. One of the tallest buildings in Asia is _____.
7. Pei added a _____ to the Louvre in Paris.

◆ MAKING INFERENCES

Circle *T* if the sentence is true and *F* if it is false. Then, underline one sentence in the passage that supports your answer.

	True	False
1. After Pei moved to the United States, he visited China very often.	T	F
2. Pei's company was always a big success.	T	F
3. Pei is famous only for his traditional designs.	T	F

◆ TELL THE STORY

Work with a partner. Tell the story of I. M. Pei to your partner. Use your own words. Your partner can ask you questions about the story. Then, your partner tells you the story and you ask questions.

DISCUSSION

Discuss the answers to these questions with your classmates.

1. Some people are afraid to be in tall buildings. Other people think tall buildings are beautiful and exciting. What do you think about tall buildings?
2. Which city do you think has beautiful architecture?
3. Many old historic buildings need additions or changes. Should architects use the original styles or more modern styles for their work?

WRITING

On a separate piece of paper, write six sentences or a short paragraph. Describe the building you live in.

Example: *I live in an apartment building. There are 56 units in the apartment building.*

UNIT 22

EVA PERÓN
(1919–1952)

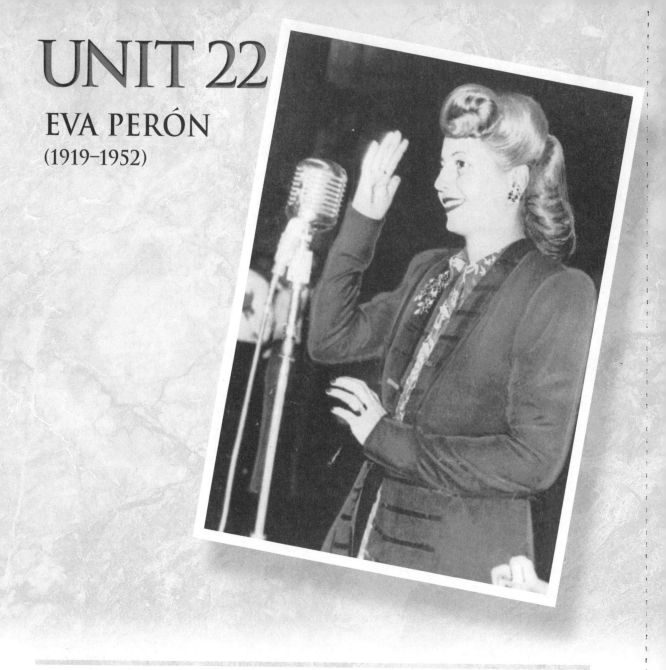

BEFORE YOU READ

Eva Perón was a poor girl who married a president. She became very powerful and was loved by millions.

Discuss these questions with a partner.

1. Who are some famous political leaders of the past or present?
2. Who is your favorite political leader? What makes this person great?
3. Look at the picture of Eva Perón. What can you say about her?

Now read about Eva Perón.

EVA PERÓN

Eva Perón was born in 1919 in a small village in Argentina. Her family was very poor. Eva always had big dreams. She wanted to be a famous actress. When she was 15 years old, she convinced a tango singer to take her to Buenos Aires, the capital city of Argentina. In Buenos Aires, Eva learned that big-city life was not easy. She had no friends, no job, and no work experience. But she was **determined to** succeed. She got small parts in radio programs and began to make money. She became well known as an actress on the radio. Soon she was a **celebrity.**

Colonel Juan Perón was Vice President and Minister of War when he and Eva met. They immediately fell in love. He was 48 years old and she was 24. Juan Perón helped Eva get better jobs. Soon she became the head of all the radio stations in Argentina. Juan Perón became President in 1946. Eva worked hard for his **election.** She gave many speeches, and many people said she was one of the best speakers in Argentina. Five days after Perón's election, he and Eva got married.

As first lady of Argentina, Eva Perón worked very hard to help Perón's government. She became head of the Ministry of Labor and Health. Some people, especially those in the upper classes, did not like her. They thought that this ordinary actress had too much power. They **accused** her of spending too much government money on herself. Eva liked to look glamorous and wore very expensive clothes. One report said she wore 306 different dresses in 207 days!

Eva Perón decided that she wanted to help poor people. She wanted to change her **image.** She wore simpler clothes. She gave food, money, and clothing to the poor. Working people loved her and called her "Evita." She built houses and hospitals for the poor and the elderly. She also worked hard for women's rights. In 1947, her work helped Argentinian women get the right to vote. But she spent a lot of the government's money. People said she spent so much money that the government was **bankrupt.**

People were obsessed with Evita. Once when she gave a speech, nine people died in the rush to see her. When she visited Spain, 3 million people greeted her. In 1950, Evita started to look tired and she fainted in public. Doctors discovered that she had cancer. Her doctor told her not to work so much, but she didn't listen. She worked hard to get her husband re-elected, and in 1951 he won the presidential election for a second time. But Eva Perón's health was getting worse. She weighed only 70 pounds. When she appeared in public, she was so weak that her husband had to help her stand up.

Eva Perón died in 1952 at the age of 33. After her death, 40,000 people signed a letter to ask the Roman Catholic Church to make her a **saint.** For 16 days, people came from all over Argentina to mourn her death and see her body. So many people came that 120,000 people were injured in one day. All the flower shops in Buenos Aires were sold out.

Eva Perón's body was dressed and made up so she looked like she did when she was alive. Juan Perón wanted to make a monument for her. He thought that this would help him to be popular again. But he soon lost power and General Pedro Eugenio Aramburu became President. Aramburu wanted people to forget about Juan and Eva Perón. He didn't allow the monument to be built and wanted to **get rid of** Eva's body.

There were many stories about what happened to Evita's body. After President Aramburu died in 1970, his lawyer gave the government information that solved the mystery. In 1971, officials opened the grave of a woman in Italy. They found the body of Eva Perón. The body had been there for 16 years. In 1976, the government buried Eva's body in her family's grave in Buenos Aires. No one will ever forget Evita, and today she is as famous as ever. Over the years, many people wrote books, songs, and plays about her life, including the famous musical play *Evita*. The legend of Evita will live forever.

VOCABULARY

◆ MEANING

Match the words with their meanings.

____ 1. image	a. having a strong desire to do something
____ 2. get rid of	b. to say someone has done something wrong
____ 3. election	c. the opinion that people have of somone
____ 4. bankrupt	d. famous person, especially an entertainer
____ 5. determined to	e. someone who the Catholic Church honors after death
____ 6. celebrity	f. to make something that is unpleasant go away
____ 7. saint	g. time when people vote to choose a political leader
____ 8. accuse	h. not having money to pay one's debts

◆ USE

Work with a partner and answer these questions. Use complete sentences.

1. How do people usually *get rid of* things they don't want anymore?
2. What are the qualities of a *saint*?
3. In what profession is *image* very important?
4. Who votes in an *election*?
5. What happens when a company goes *bankrupt*?
6. What usually happens after a person is *accused* of a crime?

COMPREHENSION

◆ UNDERSTANDING THE READING

Circle the letter of the best answer.

1. When Eva Perón arrived in Buenos Aires, she _____.
   a. was well prepared for her new life
   b. had to overcome many troubles at first
   c. became successful right away

2. Juan and Eva Perón _____.
   a. helped one another to succeed
   b. argued about Eva's power
   c. were bad for each other

3. While Eva Perón was the first lady, she _____.
   a. never thought about herself
   b. was loved by all of Argentine society
   c. both helped and hurt Argentina

◆ REMEMBERING DETAILS

Reread the passage and answer the questions.

1. Why did Eva leave her village and go to Buenos Aires?
2. What was Juan Perón's position when Eva met him?
3. When did Juan and Eva get married?
4. What government job did Eva Perón have?
5. Why did the poor people love "Evita"?
6. How long was Eva Perón's body in the grave in Italy?

◆ MAKING INFERENCES

Circle _T_ if the sentence is true and _F_ if it is false. Then, underline one sentence in the passage that supports your answer.

	True	False
1. Eva wasn't successful before she met Juan Perón.	T	F
2. Eva just wanted to enjoy life while she was the first lady.	T	F
3. People forgot about Eva after she died.	T	F

◆ TELL THE STORY

Work with a partner. Tell the story of Eva Perón to your partner. Use your own words. Your partner can ask you questions about the story. Then, your partner tells you the story and you ask questions.

DISCUSSION

Discuss the answers to these questions with your classmates.

1. Some people didn't like Eva Perón because she had so much power and spent so much money. Other people liked her because she helped the poor. What do you think about Eva Perón?

2. Do you think women are better leaders than men? Why or why not?

3. Do you think a person who does not have a formal education can become a good political leader? Why or why not?

WRITING

On a separate piece of paper, write six sentences or a short paragraph. Write about a famous world leader of the past or present.

Example: *King Abdullah II is the King of Jordan. He became King when his father died.*

UNIT 23
STEPHEN HAWKING
(1942–   )

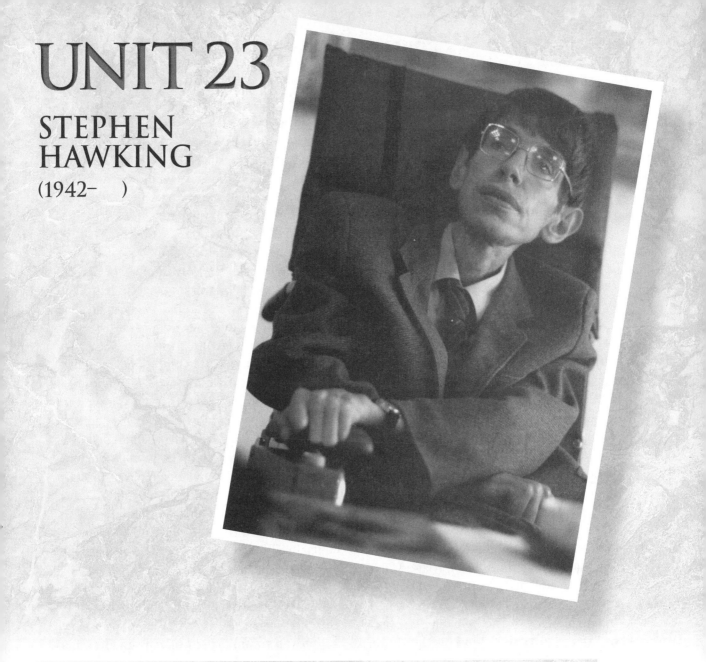

BEFORE YOU READ

Stephen Hawking is the greatest physicist since Albert Einstein. He is famous and successful, but he is also disabled.

Discuss these questions with a partner.

1. What famous people do you know with disabilities?
2. Do you think people with disabilities can have good and successful lives?
3. Look at the picture of Stephen Hawking. What can you say about him?

Now read about Stephen Hawking.

STEPHEN HAWKING

There is a man driving around in a motorized wheelchair in Cambridge, England. He can only move his eyes and two fingers on his left hand. He **communicates** through a computer. He types words on the computer and the computer speaks for him. This man is Stephen Hawking. People know him for his courage and his sense of humor. He is also the greatest physicist since Albert Einstein.

Stephen Hawking was born in 1942 in Oxford, England. His father was a specialist in tropical diseases. Stephen wanted to be a scientist too. He went to the University of Oxford and received a degree in physics. He then went to the University of Cambridge to study for a **Ph.D.** During this time doctors discovered that he had ALS, which is sometimes called Lou Gehrig's disease. This **fatal** disease weakens all of the body's muscles. Most people with ALS live for five years. The doctors thought Hawking would live for only two and a half more years. When Hawking heard this, he became very **depressed**.

At about this time he met Jane Wilde, a language student at Cambridge. They fell in love and got married in 1965. Hawking has often said that his wife gave him the courage to continue to study and work. Although Hawking had become more severely paralyzed, he became a professor at Cambridge. Luckily, the work of a physicist only requires one thing: the mind. Hawking had a son and then a daughter. He had another son 12 years later when his disease had gotten much worse. His youngest son has never heard his father's real voice. He has only heard the voice from the computer.

Hawking does **research** about how the universe began. He sees connections and works out explanations that other people cannot. His research has influenced many other scientists. Some of his ideas are so advanced that other scientists cannot prove them yet. His most famous ideas are about black holes. Black holes are not really holes. They are areas in space that are very **dense**. They are so dense that even light cannot pass through. That is why they are called black holes.

As his disease got worse, money became a problem for Stephen Hawking. He had a lot of medical expenses. He needed special wheelchairs, nurses 24 hours a day, and machines to help him read and speak. To earn extra money, Hawking gave speeches and published **articles**. Then someone told him to write a book that explained the universe to ordinary people. Hawking agreed and wrote *A Brief History of Time*. The book sold over 8 million copies worldwide, and Hawking became a millionaire. Even though most people could not understand Hawking's ideas, he amazed them. Hawking became world famous. He met the Queen of England, he was on the covers of magazines, and he appeared on television shows.

In 1990, Hawking ended his 25-year marriage. This was shocking to many of his friends because his wife, Jane, was very **devoted** to him. She took care of all of his needs. She fed him, bathed him, dressed him, and raised their children by herself. Hawking left her for a younger woman— his nurse! They were married in 1995.

Hawking's strong personality and spirit have helped him to live with ALS for over 30 years. He has helped to make people aware of ALS and other disabilities. Hawking teaches us that even though a person is physically disabled, the mind has no limits.

VOCABULARY

◆ MEANING

Write the correct words in the blanks.

| Ph.D. | devoted | dense | depressed |
| fatal | research | articles | communicate |

1. Black holes are actually filled with a lot of material. They are very _____.

2. A _____ disease, such as ALS, causes death.

3. Stephen Hawking wrote stories for newspapers and magazines. The _____ helped to pay for his medical costs.

4. Hawking cannot speak or write to share his ideas and feelings with other people. He can only _____ through a computer.

5. Hawking's wife, Jane, loved and cared for her husband. She was _____ to him.

6. Hawking studied about the universe because he wanted to find out new facts. He did a lot of _____.

7. Hawking was _____ when the doctor told him he was very sick.

8. Hawking studied for his _____, or doctorate, the highest university degree.

◆ USE

Work with a partner and answer these questions. Use complete sentences.

1. What is something that you are *devoted* to?
2. What are some of the modern machines we use to *communicate*?
3. What types of *articles* do you like to read?
4. For what kind of job does a person need a *Ph.D.*?
5. What kinds of objects are *dense*? What kinds are not?
6. How can you tell when a person is *depressed*?

COMPREHENSION

◆ UNDERSTANDING THE READING

Circle the letter of the best answer.

1. Stephen Hawking is an example of someone who _____.
   a. has overcome obstacles
   b. is devoted to his family
   c. cannot face his problems

2. The doctors who told Hawking that he had ALS _____.
   a. were wrong
   b. thought he would get better
   c. expected him to die

3. Hawking's disability _____.
   a. stopped him from doing what he loved most in life
   b. is getting better every day
   c. did not stop him from living a happy and successful life

◆ REMEMBERING DETAILS

Reread the passage and answer the questions.

1. What are the only parts of Hawking's body that he can move?
2. How does Hawking speak to people?
3. How many children does Hawking have?
4. What is Hawking's job at the University of Cambridge?
5. Where did Hawking study for his degree in physics?
6. What famous book did Hawking write?
7. How many copies of his book sold?

◆ MAKING INFERENCES

Circle *T* if the sentence is true and *F* if it is false. Then, underline one sentence in the passage that supports your answer.

	True	False
1. ALS causes problems only with the body, not the mind.	T	F
2. Hawking's book was only popular with scientists.	T	F
3. Hawking divorced his wife because she didn't help him.	T	F

◆ TELL THE STORY

Work with a partner. Tell the story of Stephen Hawking to your partner. Use your own words. Your partner can ask you questions about the story. Then, your partner tells you the story and you ask questions.

DISCUSSION

Discuss the answers to these questions with your classmates.

1. Stephen Hawking cannot speak. His computer speaks for him. How else can computers be used in the future to help people?
2. Some people believe that Hawking's strong personality has helped him to live longer than the doctors expected. Do you agree with this?
3. Do you think there is life in outer space?

WRITING

On a separate piece of paper, write six sentences or a short paragraph. Describe a person with a mental or physical disability.

Example: *My grandfather is 81 years old, and he has a problem hearing. He doesn't want to wear his hearing aid because he says it makes a noise.*

UNIT 24

ARTHUR ASHE
(1943–1993)

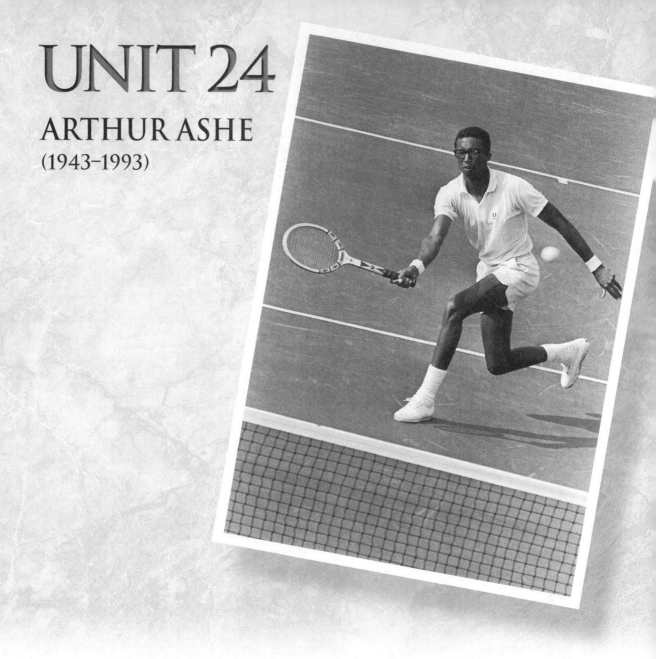

BEFORE YOU READ

Arthur Ashe was one of the first African American tennis stars.

Discuss these questions with a partner.

1. Who are some famous male tennis stars?
2. Is tennis popular in your country?
3. Do you prefer individual sports, like tennis, or team sports, like soccer?

Now read about Arthur Ashe.

ARTHUR ASHE

Arthur Ashe was one of the world's first African American tennis stars. He was a great athlete, and he won many titles. He became rich and famous, but these things never changed his good character. He never behaved badly. Ashe was **fair,** honest, and kind both in his life and on the tennis court. He also worked for many charities and always tried to help people.

Arthur Ashe was born in 1943 in Richmond, Virginia. In that part of the United States at that time, African American people and white people didn't live, play, go to school, or even eat together. Arthur's father was in charge of the city's largest park for African Americans. Arthur played there every day. He was not good at most sports. But when he was seven years old, he played tennis for the first time. He liked it and played very well. His mother had died the year before, and Arthur played every day for hours to forget his sadness.

One day, a teacher at the park noticed Arthur's ability in tennis. He took Arthur to see a tennis teacher. Arthur learned a lot from him. Arthur became an excellent amateur tennis player. He won several titles. After high school, Arthur went to St. Louis, Missouri, to train with another **coach.** At the age of 19, he was one of the best young players in the United States. Arthur won a **scholarship** to UCLA, the University of California in Los Angeles. He studied hard and graduated four years later. He also won many tennis tournaments and became the first African American man to play on the U.S. national team.

In 1969, Arthur Ashe became a professional. Six years later, he won the World Champion Tennis singles title and the Wimbledon singles title. He was the first African American man to win at Wimbledon and the first to be number one in the world. His success opened the way for African American players in tennis.

Ashe's great success did not come easily. Many times over the years he suffered because of **racism.** Sometimes, he was not allowed to play in tournaments. Other times when he played, people were unkind to him. But Ashe was always calm and well mannered. He hated bad behavior on the court. He got angry only once, when his opp_____ said bad things about him because of his race. Still, Arthur didn't say anything. He just walked off the tennis court and did not finish the game.

Ashe met a photographer at a charity event to raise money for African American schools. Later they married and had a daughter. They named her Camera. Ashe was a devoted and loving father. He also taught his daughter to be a good and kind person. Every Christmas, he took her to give toys to children from poor families. Camera gave them some of her own toys too. Ashe had a lot of money, but he never liked to **show off.** At the end of his life, he owned only five suits and five pairs of shoes.

Ashe was also very successful off the tennis court. He is the author of several books, including a complete history of African American athletes in the United States. In 1973, he received the Presidential Medal of Freedom, one of America's highest honors.

In 1979, Ashe had a heart attack. The following year, he retired from tennis. After that, he spent a lot of time helping young athletes and working for equal rights for all people. In 1983, he had heart surgery. Unfortunately, he got the **incurable** disease AIDS from blood he received in the hospital. Ashe continued to help people, even when he was very sick. Shortly before he died in 1993, he started an organization to help find a **cure** for AIDS.

VOCABULARY

◆ MEANING

Write the correct words in the blanks.

racism	cure	show off	opponent
scholarship	incurable	fair	coach

1. A _____ is a medicine or treatment that makes a disease or illness better.
2. People _____ to try and make people notice or admire them.
3. _____ is when people think their own race is better than others and others are not as good as they are.
4. A _____ is a person who trains athletes.
5. When students get a _____, they get money from an organization to help them pay for their school.
6. A player's _____ is the person on the other side or team.
7. A disease is _____ when there is no way to make it better.
8. When you treat people honestly and equally, you are _____.

◆ USE

Work with a partner and answer these questions. Use complete sentences.

1. In which job is it very important to be *fair*?
2. How do rich people sometimes *show off*?
3. What are some of the problems caused by *racism*?
4. What are some sports that you need a *coach* for?
5. Which diseases do not have *cures*?
6. How should players act toward their *opponents*?

COMPREHENSION

◆ UNDERSTANDING THE READING

Circle the letter of the best answer.

1. During tennis games, Arthur Ashe _____.
   a. wanted to win no matter what happened
   b. often lost his temper
   c. controlled his emotions

2. After Ashe became a professional, he _____.
   a. still had some problems
   b. was accepted by everyone
   c. lived a wild and exciting life

3. Ashe cared most about _____.
   a. winning titles
   b. helping people
   c. making money

◆ REMEMBERING DETAILS

Reread the passage and fill in the blanks.

1. _____ was the first person to notice Ashe's ability in tennis.

2. Ashe graduated from _____.

3. Ashe was the first African American man to play on the _____ team.

4. Ashe was the first African American man to win _____.

5. Ashe retired from tennis after he had a _____.

6. Ashe named his daughter Camera because his wife was a _____.

7. Ashe wanted to help find a cure for _____.

◆ MAKING INFERENCES

Circle *T* if the sentence is true and *F* if it is false. Then, underline one sentence in the passage that supports your answer.

	True	False
1. Ashe was not very close to his mother.	T	F
2. Possessions were not important to Ashe.	T	F
3. Ashe received awards only for playing tennis.	T	F

◆ TELL THE STORY

Work with a partner. Tell the story of Arthur Ashe to your partner. Use your own words. Your partner can ask you questions about the story. Then, your partner tells you the story and you ask questions.

DISCUSSION

Discuss the answers to these questions with your classmates.

1. What is the best way to do something about racism?
2. Arthur Ashe played tennis to forget his sadness. When you have a problem or are sad, what do you do?
3. Ashe named his daughter Camera because his wife was a photographer. Do you think it is good for parents to give their children unusual names?

WRITING

On a separate piece of paper, write six sentences or a short paragraph. Describe someone who likes to show off or someone who doesn't like to show off.

Example: *My aunt is very successful, but she doesn't like to show off. She lives a very simple life.*

ANSWER KEY

*Answers not given will vary. For **Making Inferences**, other sentences may be correct.*

Unit 1   Wolfgang Amadeus Mozart
Meaning: **1.** b **2.** c **3.** c **4.** a
5. a **6.** c **7.** b **8.** c
Understanding the Reading:
1. b **2.** a **3.** b
Remembering Details: **1.** his father, Leopold **2.** 5 years old. **3.** He was not handsome. He was a small man with a large head and pale skin.
4. Her sister did not love him. **5.** at six o'clock in the evening. **6.** over 600
Making Inferences: **1.** F: When he was six, he was already earning money for his family. **2.** F: Mozart made a lot of money, but he was always in debt.
3. T: Sadly, no one went to his funeral.

Unit 2   Dr. James Barry
Meaning: **1.** b **2.** b **3.** a **4.** a
5. b **6.** c **7.** b **8.** c
Understanding the Reading:
1. c **2.** b **3.** b
Remembering Details:
1. 20 years old **2.** 45 years
3. South Africa **4.** She saved the life of the governor's daughter. **5.** She had a reputation as a troublemaker.
6. She did not obey orders.
Making Inferences: **1.** F: In 1856 she went to South Africa, and she was soon known as the best doctor and surgeon in the colony. **2.** T: She made hospitals follow strict rules for taking care of the sick. **3.** F: If people talked about her high voice or tiny figure, she became angry.

Unit 3   Charles Dickens
Meaning: **1.** labels **2.** required
3. margin **4.** superstitious
5. series **6.** ornaments
7. routine **8.** meticulous
Understanding the Reading:
1. c. **2.** c **3.** a
Remembering Details: **1.** 15 years old **2.** *The Pickwick Papers*
3. tours **4.** the United States
5. 10 **6.** three parts **7.** touched
Making Inferences: **1.** F: Because of

his difficult childhood, he was afraid to be poor. **2.** F: Dickens wrote powerful and honest stories about the lives of poor people. **3.** T: The government even passed laws to stop some of the horrible things he wrote about in his books.

Unit 4   Alfred Nobel
Meaning: **1.** c **2.** a **3.** b **4.** h
5. e **6.** d **7.** f **8.** g
Understanding the Reading:
1. b **2.** b **3.** a
Remembering Details: **1.** a gold medal; a diploma; about $1 million
2. Russia **3.** The United States; several European countries **4.** laboratory
5. dynamite **6.** 1901
Making Inferences: **1.** F: Workers used it to build roads through mountains and to construct mines deep in the earth. **2.** F: He wanted people to remember him as a man of peace. **3.** F: He built a new laboratory and continued his work.

Unit 5   Sofia Kovalevsky
Meaning: **1.** c **2.** a **3.** a **4.** a
5. c **6.** b **7.** b **8.** a
Understanding the Reading:
1. a **2.** b **3.** c
Remembering Details: **1.** physics
2. St. Petersburg **3.** Germany **4.** She had solved a problem that was very important to science. **5.** She was the only woman to be a professor in Europe, outside of Italy.
Making Inferences: **1.** F: After five years of friendship, however, they finally fell in love. **2.** F: He began to have money and job problems. **3.** F: During these years, Sofia Kovalevsky worked completely alone.

Unit 6   Vincent van Gogh
Meaning: **1.** sorrow **2.** mental
3. encourage **4.** moody
5. scrap **6.** the country
7. stubborn **8.** chase

Understanding the Reading:
1. c **2.** c **3.** a
Remembering Details: **1.** 1881
2. first in Brussels, then in Paris
3. ordinary things: a chair, flowers
4. his brother, Theo **5.** his ear
6. almost 200 **7.** after he died
Making Inferences: **1.** F: Van Gogh's paintings were very different from paintings of other artists, and people didn't like them. **2.** T: He believed that Vincent was a genius. **3.** F: He had a strange, moody personality.

Unit 7   Maggie Walker
Meaning: **1.** members
2. financial **3.** community **4.** site
5. staff **6.** slave **7.** loans
8. establish
Understanding the Reading:
1. b **2.** a **3.** b
Remembering Details:
1. a teacher **2.** take care of the sick and bury the dead **3.** She was a woman. **4.** 3,400 **5.** $1 **6.** It named a high school, a theater, and a street after her.
Making Inferences: **1.** F: In 1907, Walker fell and was never able to walk again. **2.** T: In just a few years, it grew from 3,400 members to 50,000 members. **3.** T: St. Luke's gave them a loan and saved the school system.

Unit 8   Helena Rubinstein
Meaning: **1.** e **2.** c **3.** f **4.** g
5. b **6.** a **7.** h **8.** d
Understanding the Reading:
1. b **2.** a **3.** b
Remembering Details: **1.** doctor
2. Poland; Australia **3.** face cream
4. London; Paris **5.** "the beauty queen" **6.** prince **7.** 94
Making Inferences: **1.** F: Then he wanted her to get married, but she refused. **2.** F: She paid them very little money and they worked very hard.
3. T: Her work was the most important thing to her, and she dreamed only of expanding her business.

Unit 9   Julia Morgan

Meaning: 1. affected
2. discouraged   3. castle
4. demanding   5. extravagant
6. crooked   7. civil engineering
8. architect
Understanding the Reading:
1. b.   2. a   3. a
Remembering Details: 1. San
Simeon, California   2. math; science
3. entrance exams   4. architect's
license 5. office building   6. 20
7. traveled
Making Inferences: 1. F: Morgan
was talented and soon had a lot of
work.   2. T: She was always busy
with her work, so she didn't have
time for other interests or much of a
social life.   3. F: She was the first
woman to attend the École des Beaux-
Arts, but she was not allowed to sit
with her classmates.

Unit 10   Princess Ka'iulani

Meaning: 1. missionaries   2. ports
3. minority   4. despair   5. annex
6. dignity   7. fairy tale   8. duty
Understanding the Reading:
1. a   2. b   3. a
Remembering Details: 1. Her
uncle, King Kalakaua, did not have
children.   2. England   3. San
Francisco   4. It was a perfect place
for ports and military bases.   5. 1897
6. President Grover Cleveland
Making Inferences: 1. F: Ka'iulani
was very sad after her mother's death.
2. T: For many years, other countries
wanted to control the Hawaiian
Islands.   3. T: She was full of despair
and was too weak to fight her illness.

Unit 11   Isadora Duncan

Meaning: 1. loose   2. arts
3. threatened   4. glory   5. bad
temper   6. drowned   7. still
8. formal
Understanding the Reading:
1. b   2. c   3. c
Remembering Details: 1. She told
her that marriage was terrible.
2. Isadora's two children and their
nurse   3. 44   4. Russian
5. Nice, France   6. Her scarf got
caught in the wheel of a car and broke
her neck.
Making Inferences: 1. F: Dora

believed children should be free, so
Isadora grew up with few rules.
2. F: She was only interested in her
art.   3. F: But she never lost her
energy and her love for life.

Unit 12   Diego Rivera

Meaning: 1. b   2. a   3. c   4. a
5. a   6. a   7. c   8. b
Understanding the Reading:
1. b   2. a   3. b
Remembering Details: 1. Pablo
Picasso   2. history; traditions; culture
3. Mexico's history   4. New York City
5. stories   6. two separate houses
Making Inferences: 1. F: Rivera was
also very interested in politics.   2. T:
Rivera was a very big man.   3. F:
Many Americans were angry about
this. They destroyed the mural, and
Rivera left the United States.

Unit 13   Jim Thorpe

Meaning: 1. d   2. g   3. f   4. h
5. a   6. e   7. b   8. c
Understanding the Reading:
1. b   2. b   3. b
Remembering Details: 1. fish; hunt;
swim   2. 16   3. gold medals   4. less
than a year   5. baseball; football
6. 30 years
Making Inferences: 1. T: He was a
star athlete in several sports, including
baseball, running, wrestling, and
football.   2. F: Many people tried to
get Thorpe's medals back to him.
3. T: He had several jobs and also gave
speeches on sports and Native
American issues.

Unit 14   Agatha Christie

Meaning: 1. c   2. a   3. a
4. c   5. b   6. c   7. c   8. a
Understanding the Reading:
1. b   2. c   3. c
Remembering Details: 1. *The
Murder of Roger Ackroyd*   2. coat
3. archeologist   4. Christmas
5. nurse   6. a small village   7. died
Making Inferences: 1. F: Readers
loved the characters of Miss Marple
and Hercule Poirot and always wanted
to read their next cases.   2. T: She is
very bright and always solves the
crimes before the police do.   3. F:
Her books still continue to sell.

Unit 15   Louis Armstrong

Meaning: 1. mourn   2. nonsense
3. idol   4. opportunity   5. run-down
6. arrest   7. aware of   8. modest
Understanding the Reading:
1. b   2. a   3. c
Remembering Details: 1. He fired a
gun into the air.   2. Chicago
3. 1925   4. *Hot Chocolate*   5. His
mouth was as big as a large satchel.
6. King George VI   7. over 2,000
Making Inferences: 1. F: At the
home, Louis learned to play the
cornet, a musical instrument that is
like a trumpet.   2. T: In 1922, "King"
Oliver asked Armstrong to join him in
Chicago. It was a great opportunity for
Armstrong.   3. F: People around the
world wanted to hear Louis
Armstrong.

Unit 16   Umm Kulthum

Meaning: 1. b   2. a   3. a   4. c
5. b   6. a   7. b   8. c
Understanding the Reading:
1. c   2. c   3. a
Remembering Details: 1. to earn
extra money   2. religious songs   3. on
the first Thursday of every month   4. a
silk handkerchief   5. two   6. 4 million
Making Inferences: 1. F: She hired
teachers, took lessons, and practiced.
2. T: Umm and her father began to
earn a lot of money.   3. F: Umm
Kulthum's career really started when
she began to make records.

Unit 17 Howard Hughes

Meaning: 1. d   2. f   3. a
4. h   5. c   6. g   7. e   8. b
Understanding the Reading:
1. b   2. c   3. b
Remembering Details: 1. Hughes
Tool Company   2. Los Angeles,
California   3. plane crashed
4. favorite room   5. his name; simple
jobs   6. a steak; a baked potato; 12
peas   7. same room
Making Inferences: 1. F: He set many
flying records, including the fastest
flight around the world at the time.
2. F: He worked hard, but he also
played hard.   3. F: Hughes used
people for his pleasure and didn't treat
them very well, so he had no real
friends.

Unit 18   Soichiro Honda
Meaning: **1.** give up   **2.** ad
3. competitive   **4.** reliable
5. crushed   **6.** begged
7. tremendously   **8.** amazed
Understanding the Reading:
1. c   **2.** b   **3.** b
Remembering Details: **1.** Tokyo
2. it crashed   **3.** 1948   **4.** It was
lightweight.   **5.** "You Meet the Nicest
People on a Honda"   **6.** 1 million
7. The Honda Civic, the Accord, and
the Prelude
Making Inferences: **1.** T: He started
the company with only $3,300.   **2.** F:
The company sold thousands of
motorcycles to new riders.   **3.** F: He
believed that workers and bosses
should have a close relationship.

Unit 19   Mother Teresa
Meaning: **1.** c   **2.** f   **3.** d   **4.** e
5. g   **6.** h   **7.** a   **8.** b
Understanding the Reading:
1. c   **2.** a   **3.** a
Remembering Details: **1.** India
2. 20 years   **3.** a hospital   **4.** the
Missionaries of Charity   **5.** white
cotton saris   **6.** She was poor.
7. the Nobel Peace Prize
Making Inferences: **1.** F: Agnes
often went with her, and she enjoyed
helping these people.   **2.** F: The
school had no roof, no walls, and no
chairs.   **3.** F: But she always said her
greatest reward was helping people.

Unit 20   Sonja Henie
Meaning: **1.** train   **2.** tough
3. glamour   **4.** raw   **5.** represent
6. spectacular   **7.** diet
8. introduce
Understanding the Reading:
1. c   **2.** b   **3.** a
Remembering Details: **1.** 11 years
old   **2.** a gold medal; two more gold
medals   **3.** beautiful; short; white

4. glamorous; spectacular   **5.** long
hours   **6.** raw eggs; raw beef   **7.** white
Rolls Royce; mansion
Making Inferences: **1.** F: Her movie
fans went to her ice shows and her
skating fans went to her movies.
2. T: Henie liked people to know that
she was rich.   **3.** F: Henie worked
hard for her money.

Unit 21   I. M. Pei
Meaning: **1.** a   **2.** c   **3.** c   **4.** b
5. b   **6.** b   **7.** b   **8.** c
Understanding the Reading:
1. c   **2.** a   **3.** c
Remembering Details: **1.** Canton,
China   **2.** engineering; architecture
3. safely destroy buildings
4. mountains   **5.** windows   **6.** the
Bank of China building in Hong Kong
7. pyramid
Making Inferences: **1.** F: In 1974, he
visited China for the first time in 40
years.   **2.** F: After a while, his company
lost a lot of business.   **3.** F: Pei added a
glass and steel pyramid to the 700-year-
old building. This was unusual, because
the Louvre is a traditional building and
the pyramid is modern.

Unit 22   Eva Perón
Meaning: **1.** c   **2.** f   **3.** g   **4.** h
5. a   **6.** d   **7.** e   **8.** b
Understanding the Reading:
1. b   **2.** a   **3.** c
Remembering Details:
1. to be a famous actress   **2.** Vice
President and Minister of War
3. 1946   **4.** the head of the Ministry
of Labor and Health   **5.** She gave
food, money, and clothing to the poor
6. 16 years
Making Inferences: **1.** F: She
became well known as an actress on
the radio.   **2.** F: As first lady of
Argentina, Eva Perón worked very
hard to help Perón's government.

3. F: No one will ever forget Evita,
and today she is as famous as ever.

Unit 23   Stephen Hawking
Meaning: **1.** dense   **2.** fatal
3. articles   **4.** communicate
5. devoted   **6.** research
7. depressed   **8.** Ph.D.
Understanding the Reading:
1. a   **2.** c   **3.** c
Remembering Details: **1.** his eyes
and two fingers on his left hand
2. through a computer   **3.** 3
4. a professor   **5.** Oxford
6. *A Brief History of Time*   **7.** over 8
million
Making Inferences: **1.** T: Although
Hawking had become more severely
paralyzed, he became a professor at
Cambridge.   **2.** F: Then someone told
him to write a book that explained the
universe to ordinary people.   **3.** F:
This was shocking to many of his
friends because his wife, Jane, was very
devoted to him.

Unit 24   Arthur Ashe
Meaning: **1.** cure   **2.** show off
3. racism   **4.** coach
5. scholarship   **6.** opponent
7. incurable   **8.** fair
Understanding the Reading:
1. c   **2.** a   **3.** b
Remembering Details: **1.** a teacher
2. UCLA   **3.** U.S. national
4. at Wimbledon   **5.** heart attack
6. photographer   **7.** AIDS
Making Inferences: **1.** F: His mother
had died the year before, and Arthur
played every day for hours to forget
his sadness.   **2.** T: At the end of his
life, he owned only five suits and five
pairs of shoes.   **3.** F: In 1973, he
received the Presidential Medal of
Freedom, one of America's highest
honors.

BIBLIOGRAPHY

Bryant, Mark. *Private Lives: Curious Facts about the Famous and Infamous.* London: Cassell, 1998.

Chipman, Dawn, Mari Florence, and Naomi Wax. *Cool Women.* Los Angeles: Girl Press, 1998.

Christ, Henry. *Globe World Biographies.* Upper Saddle River, NJ: Globe Fearon, 1987.

Forbes, Malcolm, and Jeff Bloch. *Women Who Made a Difference.* New York: Simon & Schuster, 1990.

Hahn, Emma. *16 Extraordinary American Women.* Portland, ME: J. Weston Walch, Publishers, 1996.

http://www.brittanica.com. Chicago: Brittanica.com Inc.

Ignus, Tayomi, et al. *Book of Black Heroes: Great Women in the Struggle.* East Orange, NJ: Just Us Books, Inc., 1991.

Kehoe, John. Lifefile: Howard Hughes *Biography Magazine* Jan. 1998.

Krull, Kathleen. *Lives of the Artists: Masterpieces, Messes (And What the Neighbors Thought).* San Diego: Harcourt Trade Publishers, 1995.

Krull, Kathleen. *Lives of the Athletes: Thrills, Spills (And What the Neighbors Thought).* San Diego: Harcourt Trade Publishers, 1997.

Krull, Kathleen. *Lives of the Musicians: Good Times, Bad Times (And What the Neighbors Thought).* San Diego: Harcourt Trade Publishers, 1993.

Krull, Kathleen. *Lives of the Writers: Comedies, Tragedies (And What the Neighbors Thought).* San Diego: Harcourt Trade Publishers, 1993.

Landrum, Gene N. *Profiles of Power and Success: Fourteen Geniuses Who Broke the Rules.* Amherst, NY: Prometheus Books, 1996.

Lobb, Nancy. *16 Extraordinary Asian Americans.* Portland: ME: J. Weston Walch, Publishers, 1996.

Marlow, Joan. *The Great Women.* New York: A & W Publishers, Inc. / Hart Associates, 1979.

Perl, Teri, and Analee Nunan. *Women and Numbers: Lives of Women Mathematicians Plus Discovery Activities.* San Carlos, CA: Wide World Publishing/Tetra, 1993.

Rediger, Pat. *Great African Americans in Business.* Calgary: Weigl Educational Publishers, 1996.

Rediger, Pat. *Great African Americans in Sports Series.* Calgary: Weigl Educational Publishers, 1996.

Sicherman, Barbara, and Carol Hurd Green, eds. *Notable American Women: The Modern Period.* Cambridge, MA: The Belknap Press of Harvard University Press, 1980.

Smith, Pohla. *Superstars of Women's Figure Skating (Female Sports Stars).* Broomall, PA: Chelsea House Publishers, 1998.

Strait, Raymond, and Leif Henie. *Queen of Ice, Queen of Shadows: The Unsuspected Life of Sonja Henie.* New York: Stein and Day, 1985.

Stanley, Fay. *The Last Princess: The Story of Princess Ka'iulani of Hawaii.* New York: Four Winds Press, 1991.

Traub, Carol G. *Philanthropists and Their Legacies.* Minneapolis, MN: The Oliver Press, Inc., 1997.

Webster's Dictionary of American Women. New York: Smithmark Publishers, 1996.

Welden, Amelie. *Girls Who Rocked the World: Heroines from Sacajawea to Sheryl Swoopes.* Hillsboro, OR: Beyond Words, 1998.